ATHENS

THE HIDDEN GEMS

Helen Partovi-Fraser

www.loveathens.com

Copyright 2015 Helen Partovi-Fraser
www.loveathens.com

The moral right of the author has been asserted.

All rights reserved. Apart from any fair dealing for the purposes of research or private study, or criticism or review, as permitted under the Copyright, Designs and Patents Act 1988, this publication may only be reproduced, stored or transmitted, in any form or by any means, with the prior permission in writing of the copyright owner, or in the case of the reprographic reproduction in accordance with the terms of licences issued by the Copyright Licensing Agency. Enquiries concerning reproduction outside those terms should be sent to the publisher.

Plan of the Acropolis courtesy of Author
Madmedia/permission=CC-A-5A-20

Print Edition

British Library Cataloguing in Publication Data.
A catalogue record for this book is available from the British Library.

For Leila, Laura and Lewis Partovi

'Know that our city has the greatest name amongst all men because she never yields to misfortune... And even should we ever be compelled to yield a little, for it is nature's way that all things bloom to suffer loss, there will abide a memory that we made our dwelling place to be a city endowed with all things, and the mightiest of all.'

Thucydides

'Through her love and knowledge of the city, she vividly brings Athens and her people to life, as we saunter through its bustling streets and monuments.'

Vivien Vernede

Contents

Map of Athens 8
Plan of the Acropolis 9
Acknowledgements 10
Preface 11
1. Athens Today: a Glimpse 17
2. A Nostalgic Walk 21
3. Mysteries of the Acropolis 31
4. Ancient Agora and the Temple of Hephaistos, God of Fire 45
5. Roman Forum, Hadrian's Library, Monastiraki and Zorba's Dance 57
6. Hadrian's City, a Greek Orthodox Baptism and Byzantine Museum 79
7. Byzantine Athens 91
8. Easter in Plaka 99
9. The Modern Boulevards and Wonders of the National Museum 109
10. Daphne Monastery Mosaics 123
References 132
Bibliography 133
Photographic Sources 137
The Author 139

Map of Athens

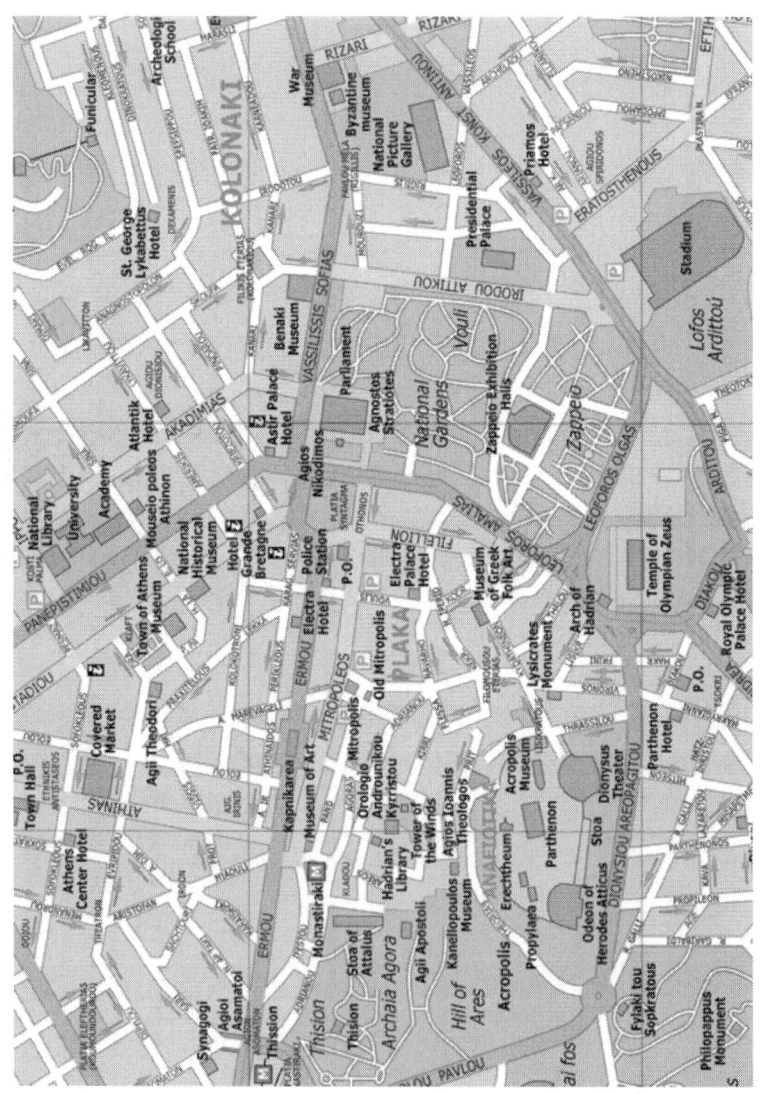

Plan of the Acropolis

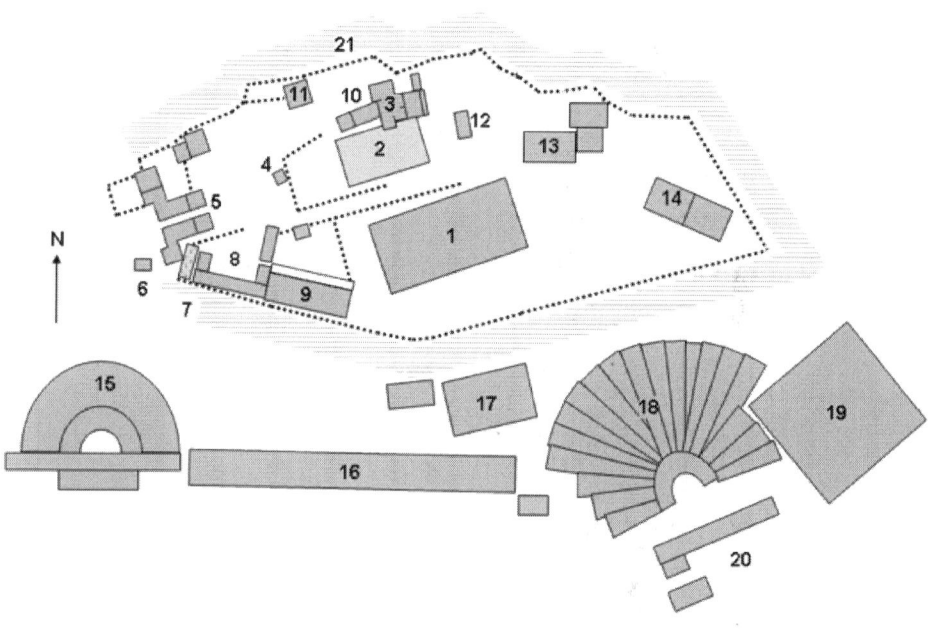

1. Parthenon
2. Old Temple of Athena
3. Erechtheion
4. Statue of Athena Promachos
5. Propylaia
6. Temple of Athena Nike
7. Eleusinian
8. Brauronion
9. Chalkotheke
10. Pandroseion
11. Arrephorion
12. Altar of Athena
13. Zeus Poleius Sanctuary
14. Pandion Sanctuary
15. Odeion of Herodes Atticus
16. Stoa of Eumenes
17. Asclepeion
18. Theatre of Dionysos
19. Odeion of Pericles
20. Sanctuary of Dionysos
21. Aglaureion

Acknowledgements

With special thanks to Laura Partovi who
accompanied me on these walks.
and
Many thanks for the services of:
The British Library
The Library of the British School at Athens
Institute of Classical Studies Library, Senate House
Friends of the British School at Athens
Stephanie Hale, of Oxford Literary Consultancy
And the Assistance of:
Leila Partovi
Lewis Partovi
Sam Vernede
and:
The People of Athens

I am also grateful to Princeton University Press for kind permission to quote from *C.P. Cavafy: Ionic* © 1972 Edmund Keeley and Philip Sherrard.

Cover design is courtesy of Oxford Literary Consultancy.

Preface

It was tantalising. Driving down through northern Greece in the summer, we passed Mount Olympus, its peaks hidden in mist. Home of the ancient gods, haunt of the sun god Apollo, the sight of laurel trees shimmering on the banks of the stream below fired my imagination. In my mind's eye I saw images of the lyre-playing god walking the slopes, and ancients in robes picking laurels to crown the winners of the ancient Games. I was transformed back to my childhood and a world of storytelling and Greek myth.

Such was my introduction to Greece, but my interest in the Hellenic world stems from a childhood part-spent awaiting my father's hastily written postcards from remote, archaeological digs. The stamps, with their images of seated gods and goddesses, became etched in my memory. Byzantine monasteries bounded by bare mountains, walls covered in mosaic, lodged in my mind and sparked an unending curiosity in the ancient Greek and Byzantine world.

Following abolition of the monarchy in 1974, Greece rapidly absorbed mass tourism and became Westernised. Membership of the EU in 1981 and the 2004 Athens Olympics were accompanied by investment in a new airport and modernisation of the public transport network. With globalisation and rapid industrialisation, international hotel chains mushroomed. Adoption in 2001 of the euro and the 2009 opening of the new Acropolis Museum finally bolstered Greece's international profile.

Over time old Athenian neighbourhoods have given way to modern, apartment blocks, and the once clearly defined roles of men and women have been weakened by women's liberation. Irregular migration, growing crime and the economic crisis have taken their toll on Athens; no longer the city of the drachma, she has become the city of the ailing euro. Soaring youth unemployment and financial meltdown have spelt unintended consequences on the social fabric of the city.

However, Greece is rebuilding its image. The Greek Orthodox Church and the tightly knit family unit continue to play a major role in the daily life of the communities. The emergence of volunteering charities and children's homes (once a rarity in Greece) reflect the Greek ability to pull together in times of hardship. And still, the Greek language, national pride and people's zest for life prevail.

A mountain of literature has been written about Athens since the Roman historian, Pausanius, wandered through the city's monuments over 2000 years ago. Since that time historians and architects, generals, politicians, poets and philosophers have walked the streets of the city in search of its secrets. After my father's death in 2007 I set out with my daughter, Laura, in the turmoil of modern Athens, in the noise, traffic and heat, to rediscover the secrets of this vibrant city. The book is not a melancholy journey in search of the past, nor does it aim to discover anything new. Rather its purpose is to stimulate interest in the history of the capital and its mix of cultures, emphasising the city's Classical heritage and overlooked Byzantine period (AD 364-1205).

The spring walks are organised roughly chronologically, taking in the Graeco-Roman era (508 BC-AD 267), moving on through the Christian period, touching the Crusader and Ottoman eras, and concluding with modern Athens (post-independence, 1830). The last chapter (10) describes a visit to the Byzantine mosaics of Daphne Monastery, a half-hour drive from the city.

It is hoped that this travel memoir, intended to accompany a standard guide book, will persuade the visitor to stay longer than 'a day or two' in Athens and enjoy its fascinating blend of old and new.

In Memory of P.M. Fraser

1. Athens Today: a Glimpse

We descend again in early light over azure sea towards new Athens airport. Along the coast mountains roll down over the plains of corn and tobacco, through olive groves and vineyards, over the curving bays of the Aegean towards Piraeus and the Saronic Gulf. With a strong tradition of sea-trading, the Athenian people have always drawn their strength from the sea and countryside, the sea imparting the city's joyous citizens with vigour and toughness, the country providing the food. Far beneath us, as the lights of the city still flicker, the *bouzouki* clubs of Glyfada have begun to empty of boisterous Athenians and the last diners have left the marinas of Vouliagmeni.

A sophisticated network of escalators, enhanced by the background beat of orchestral music, meets us on landing. We exit the airport beneath a flyover; bright yellow taxis with sparkling mirrors wait in an orderly fashion; dazed travellers queue at evenly spaced bus stops. A far cry from the old, pine-smelling Ellenikon with its crackling Zorba sound tracks and squealing seabirds, the new airport speaks of super-efficiency. Buoyant Greeks greet their loved ones with high-pitched cries, their shrieks resonating through the air. Beyond lies Mount Hymettos, recumbent, curving towards the sea.

Boarding a bus crammed with passengers, we head along a six-lane motorway, before turning into the road to Athens. Hymettos, its pure, unbroken line, boundless, its light and folds ushering in the first, rose light of Athens. Land of wild flowers, thyme and honey, homeland of monks and hermits, where 2500 years ago villagers, waiting for rain, made offerings at the shrine of Zeus.

Furniture and auto-repair shops line a cheerless road, its architecture changing as we approach the capital. It becomes tree-lined Vasilissis Sophias Avenue and the landscape of modern Athens emerges: Byzantine churches and hospitals dotted with palms; the 1971 Athens Tower, tallest building in Greece; the American Embassy, alongside Megaron Concert Hall; Eleftherios Park; and the crescent-shaped Hilton, in 1963, Athens' first high-rise. We pass the National Art Gallery, Evangelismos Hospital and the Art Deco style Officers' Club. Museums and nineteenth-century grand mansions with porches and heavy wrought iron balconies come into view. On past the embassies and houses of fashionable Kolonaki and, next to the British Embassy, the neo-Byzantine church of St Nicholas of the Poorhouse .

Athens, the European city, is unfolding before our eyes. Conceived after independence in 1829, still a small

Turkish town in 1835, the new capital was planned by Greek and Bavarian architects whose purpose was to build the most beautiful city. They adopted the style of European neoclassicism, reviving the features of Classical architecture.

Increasing traffic slows our journey but, at last, nearing Syntagma Square, we spot the roadside flower-sellers as the pale ochre façade of the Hellenic Parliament comes into view. Syntagma, heart of modern Athens, where in 1843 the people of Athens protested outside the royal palace and demanded a Constitution. Sounds of loudspeakers and crackling microphones speak of a demonstration now. Craning our necks as the bus rounds the square, we look out for Papaspirou's, the old pavement café with rickety, iron tables, now an upmarket MacDonald's. Early-rising Athenians scour daily newspapers and sip coffee around the peripteros, or kiosks. Smart Athenian girls clasping Gucci carrier bags walk hurriedly by. Life-giving rays of the early morning sun gild the solar panels of tall office blocks. The square gleams in the early light, the sun's rays dancing on blue and white national flags. Orange blossom and silver-branched olives flicker, cooled by fountains.

Disembarking onto the square, within touching distance of the Grande Bretagne, we are greeted by lottery sellers' cries and the smell of fresh, warm tyropita and koulouria, Greek cheese pies and sesame bread rings. The gaiety of the Greek square has, at this early hour, already cast its spell.

2. A Nostalgic Walk

Starting from the Hellenic Parliament in Syntagma Square, we make our way towards the Hill of the Nine Muses, Philopappou Hill, named after a first-century Roman benefactor. We amble along noisy Amalias Avenue, past the National Gardens, to glimpse again the temple of Olympeian Zeus (Olympeion)and the Arch of Hadrian. Oblivious to roaring traffic, we stroll past traders' stalls. An old periptero, its awnings covering piles of newspapers and trinkets, the owner barely visible behind a small hatch, stands unrelenting to progress. History is everywhere here; amidst the screeching of cars and shouting of street vendors, we stumble, in the dust and shadows, upon modern busts of the ancient Greek tragedians, Aeschylus, Sophocles and Euripides. I stop to look at the distant stares of these men who wrote of the ceaseless struggles between man and fate. We wander past underground Roman baths, where scents of early summer flowers and diesel intermingle. The pulse of

Athenian life is almost tangible.

Reaching a gridlocked junction, on the far side through the pines we spot again Hadrian's Arch. Today, all but brushed by rattling wires of passing trolleys, it lies on an ancient road that linked Emperor Hadrian's new Roman city to the old town of Athens. Beyond stand the remaining 15 columns of the Olympeion, one of the largest temples in the ancient Greek world. Sun-bleached columns, speaking of lost worlds, rise against blue sky. Deafened by the roar of traffic and dazzled by the morning sun, with trepidation we cross Amalias towards Dionysiou Areopagitou, now a wide, cobblestone promenade buzzing with strollers and Greek café life. A narrow road choked with traffic a few decades ago, this path takes us past pavement eateries and souvenir shops beneath the Acropolis slopes. Pausing at a statue of the unlettered, revolutionary hero General Makriyiannis, I recall the words in his book *Memoirs* (1966) that, to live honourably, men must be prepared to make sacrifices for their country.

Passing beneath the Acropolis, we refresh ourselves with a cool drink before leaving the crowds and continuing up a paved path into the woods. Amongst the pines sits the tiny chapel of St Dimitrios Loumbardiaris, a small fifteenth-century church built during the Ottoman occupation. Tradition states that the chapel was saved from extinction by a miracle: a canon directed from the Propylaia on the Acropolis had been aimed at the Christian congregation on the saint's feast day. The worshippers were saved when a thunderbolt fell on the

Propylaia, killing the commander and his family.

Accompanied by the fragrant scent of pine and soft chirring of cicadas, we climb the path up through the woods, past caves and the so-called prison of Socrates. We at last emerge into a clearing looking across the Athenian plain to the Acropolis. Ransacked by invading Persians nearly 2500 years ago, when the temples were burnt to the ground, the rocky plateau was commissioned and beautified by Pericles, Athenian orator and statesman, at the end of the Persian Wars. We reach the monumental, semicircular tomb of Philopappos, a prominent Syrian prince, Roman benefactor and consul, depicted on his tomb riding a chariot as an Athenian citizen, flanked by ancestors. Built during the reign of Emperor Hadrian to face the Parthenon, two inscriptions – one in Latin giving the public career of the benefactor and the other in Greek revealing his princely titles - reflect the cosmopolitan culture in Roman Athens.

In awe we scan the view across the plain to the mountains and glistening sea beyond. In the distance, far beyond the solar-panelled rooftops of the suburbs, stretches the port of Piraeus in the bluish haze of the Saronic Gulf. In those narrow straits in 480 BC thousands of Persian sailors were outsmarted by a few hundred Greeks. In the stillness it seems one can almost hear the echoing cries of Xerxes, the Persian king, watching helpless from a nearby hill as his ships and men sink. In this melée the poet Aeschylus fought too, describing the scene in his tragedy *The Persians* where the Persian Queen was warned that the Greeks fought as free men to defend what was precious to them. Two thousand years later in 1687 the then intact Parthenon was blown up by Venetian mercenaries, leaving it as it is today, roofless.

Slowly we make our way back down past Pnyx Hill, meeting place of the great orators and citizens of ancient Athens, and home of the first Democratic Assembly of 508 BC. Ahead rises the Areopagus, first Supreme Court of Athens, where Orestes was tried for the murder of his mother Clytemnestra and her lover. In the first century AD, 500 years after the Parthenon was built, St Paul preached to the Athenians here and on this same hill lie the ruins of the sixteenth-century church of St Dionysios who, on hearing the apostle's sermon, converted to Christianity and became first bishop and patron saint of the city.

~~~

After lunching in one of many cafés on Dionysiou Areopagitou, we stroll towards the South slope of the Acropolis and the ruins of the sanctuary of Dionysos, ancient Greek god of wine and revelry, patron of drama. It was in the ancient sanctuary here that Dionysos was first honoured with a singing and dancing chorus in the city. And here the dramatic competitions of the religious festival, City Dionysia, took place. In the original 16,000-seater stone theatre, part of which later became a single-aisle basilica with cemetery, tragic and comic plays of the Athenian tragedians and playwrights were first performed, to become a main source of leisure for Athenians, and the foundation of Western literary culture.

Converted by the Romans for gladiatorial spectacles and wild beast shows, these shattered stones breathe antiquity: the sculptural frieze created by the Romans depicts the exploits of the wine god; silent, pulsating with life, slabs of the marble barrier built to protect enthralled spectators remain. 67 high-backed, marble officials' thrones survive and in the centre sits the throne of the priest of Dionysos, carved with lion's claw feet and adorned with carvings of satyrs and grapes, symbols of rebirth. To the priest's right sat the representative of the Delphi oracle and just behind lies the seat of Hadrian, philhellene Roman Emperor.

What a location! Embedded in the hillside beneath goddess Athena's citadel, just below the ancient pathway, the theatre would have overlooked a parched Attic plain, surrounded by bare mountains and distant sea. Above the theatre lie the ruins of the 420 BC Asklepeion, sanctuary of the ancient healing god, Asklepios. Here pilgrims flocked to be healed. The sick, purified with water from a sacred spring, offered sacrifices at an altar and received advice from the god in dreams. Passed down stories from primitive man, Greek myths formed the basis of ancient Greek religion and established the deities with superhuman powers and human weaknesses. Legend holds that Asklepios, reprimanded by Zeus for restoring the dead to life, was banished and set amongst the stars above.

The sanctuary stayed open till the fifth century AD, when the shrine was converted to the church of 'Penniless Saints' (Ayii Anargyri), Cosmas and Damian, Arabian patron saints of healing, martyred by Emperor Diocletian. Surviving votive offerings from the sanctuaries of Asklepios and Dionysos, displayed in the main hall of the Acropolis Museum, reflect the vital part these healing centres played in the religious life of the ancient city. Pilgrims would have breathed clear mountain air and seen the hills of Salamis in the distance. Behind the theatre, a path leads up to a cave built around a sacred spring. Formerly a cavern dedicated to Dionysos, set up below the now-ruined choragic monument of Thrasyllus, it was transformed into the chapel of Our Lady of the Cavern (Panayia Chrysospiliotissa). During Turkish rule, Christian worship continued here and faded Byzantine frescoes and icons adorn the walls. During the 1826 siege of the Acropolis, General Makriyiannis and his men held this cave against the Turks. Nearby lies the tiny reconstructed chapel of St George of Alexandria, replacing an original, which was destroyed during the siege.

Further along, past the Theatre of Dionysos, runs the Stoa of Eumenes, a colonnaded passageway where spectators could seek shelter from the sun and stretch their legs. This path led to the (later) Odeon of Herodes Atticus, a semicircular, three-storey Roman concert hall built into the hillside. Founded by wealthy Roman consul and rich Athenian, Herodes Atticus, after the death of his young wife Regilla, the theatre was decorated throughout with marble and mosaic (of which traces remain), and is now used for theatrical performances in the annual Athens Summer Festival.

~~~

Not far away, up Byron Street, in Lysikratous Square, stands the choragic Monument of Lysikrates, a columned, marble rotunda which supported a bronze tripod awarded to the chorus leader of the winning play in the annual Dionysia. The monument sits on the route to the ancient theatre taken by the winning choruses in the Panathenaic processional route. Incorporated in the seventeenth century into a French monastery, which was later burnt down, the monument was at the time used as a reading room by the monks. Romantic writer and philhellene Lord Byron lodged here in 1810, before going on to promote the Greek War of Independence, which later led to the birth of the modern Greek nation.

Amidst the crying of street salesmen and constant revving of motorcycles, we make our way gingerly across the square. Near a busy periptero sits the church of St Catherine (Ayia Aikaterini) who, spurning the advances and offer of marriage by Emperor Maximinus, was tortured and martyred. A strong sense of neighbourhood prevails: locals with faces and expressions reminiscent of the East sit in the shade, debating the country's political misfortunes; sharp-eyed, eager-faced men roll *kolomboi* beads to while away the time; raised voices and muffled laughter resonate from the nearby garden of the Diogenes taverna. Noticing that some palm trees present during our last stroll here have vanished, I show my surprise to the periptero keeper and others nearby. 'They're not important', they shrug in the rational, seemingly unconcerned but chivalrous, way of Greeks.

The bustle of the square fades as we descend to the

stillness of the church garden. Very little documentation on these churches has survived, but we know that in the seventeenth century there were about 300 Byzantine places of worship in Athens. Dedicated to St Catherine of Alexandria and attached to the monastery of St Catherine in Sinai, this eleventh-century, popular parish church is now sunken below ground. Shaded by palms and olives, a Byzantine dome rises above a reconstructed façade of Byzantine-style arches, the continuity of religious life and traditions of the Orthodox Christian faith clearly visible in the architectural additions and extensions: only the dome, apses and roof area survive of the original Byzantine brickwork, yet the spirit of the place, the peace of the cloisters, lingers in this pretty garden.

Expressions of man's desire to worship the one God in heavenly warmth and splendour, exteriors of mid-Byzantine churches were not built to impress: their power was traditionally spiritual, radiating from within the dome. Introduced during the reign of Emperor Justinian into Constantinople, capital of Christendom, the dome of the church and its decoration, as seen in St Sophia, Church of Divine Wisdom, were conceived as a whole, replacing the traditional, flat-roofed domes of basilicas.

As evening descends we slowly stroll up the steep, whitewashed lanes of Anafiotika, the hum of the city below growing faint and distant as we cross the donkeywide paths. A settlement of white houses hidden in the rock of the Acropolis, this remote 'island' was put together by masons, who came to Athens in the nineteenth century from the island of Anafi, to help build the palace for the new king. Built in the style of a Cycladic island, amongst stepped lanes sit tiny, pure white, cubic houses with blue shutters and doors, and little courtyards filled with pink oleander, clay pots of narcissi and sweet-smelling chamomile. Siesta hour now over, shutters slowly begin to open and voices sound from within. Dozy cats stir and emerge bleary-eyed. From balconies and flat roof-tops, trailing vines and jasmine spill down whitewashed walls, their sweet scents filling the clean air.

Leaving Anafiotika behind, we head back down the steep paths, past the old Turkish baths to the lower town, where ambling, carefree crowds throng the streets. The smell of crisply fried *kalamarakia*, little squid, drifts from a local tavern. We are reminded that we are in Holy Week when Greeks fast, and many eating places do not offer meat or fish. As we sit down under a vine to enjoy a small glass of ouzo and *mezedakia,* plates of small delicacies, the sun dips behind the columns of the Parthenon, the clear blue sky ablaze in Apollo's warm, golden glow.

3. Mysteries of the Acropolis

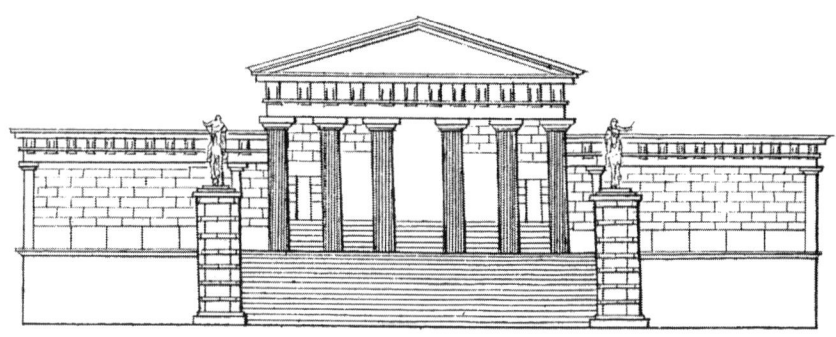

Ionic

*That we've broken their statues,
that we've driven them out of their temples,
doesn't mean at all that the gods are dead.
O land of Ionia, they're still in love with you,
Their souls still keep your memory.
When an August dawn wakes over you,
your atmosphere is potent with their life,
And sometimes a young ethereal figure,
Indistinct, in rapid flight
Wings across your hills.*

Constantine Cavafy - Ionic 1911
Translated by Edmund Keeley and Philip Sherrard.

Climbing the steep slope of the Acropolis, up the Roman steps of the grand Propylaia, the bare rock of the

Acropolis opens up before us. Symbol of power, it served as fortress, shrine and treasury. Desolate, scattered marble blocks and half-lost fragments lie strewn on the ground. To our left below, rises the Areopagus, traces of the stone steps of the open-air council of justice still visible. Spotting the small temple of Athena Nike high up on the bastion to our right, we recognise the rock where, according to legend, old King Aegeus had watched and waited for the return of his son Theseus from fighting the Minotaur. On seeing a black sail and mistakenly believing his son to be dead, the old king, stricken with grief, fell to his death below, the sea thereafter named the Aegean.

Monumental porch and grand entrance hall, its marble columns wide enough for sacrificial animals to pass, the ancient Periclean Propylaia, Roman writer Pausanius tells us, were brightly painted and roofed with marble. Designed by the greatest, then unknown, architect Mnesicles after completion of the Parthenon in 438 BC, five Doric gateways open onto a central hall with side wings, the left side once flanked with a picture gallery. Built on uneven, sloping rock, the central chamber leads on to the Panathenaic Way and the interior sanctuary of the Acropolis. Converted into Christian chapels between the sixth and tenth centuries, the Propylaia were eventually used to house Greek Orthodox archbishops. With the arrival of the Crusades in 1205, the gateway was ransacked and transformed into a Renaissance two-storey, ducal palace with marble columns and a coffered marble ceiling. A high watchtower was erected in the South wing of the Propylaia, before becoming, under the Ottomans, home to the Turkish governor.

The Parthenon, glimpsed through the columns of the Propylaia, unfolds her north and west wings before us. Built of Pentelic marble by the Athenian people, it replaced an earlier temple destroyed in the 480 BC Persian invasion. Outlined against clear blue sky, the damaged temple combines Grecian purity and simplicity, enhanced by barren mountains beyond. Exterior decoration, originally brightly painted, would have overawed visitors. The west entrance, now despoiled of the sculpture which filled its pediment, displayed a scene from goddess Athena's contest with Poseidon, Greek god of the sea, for supremacy over Athens.

Designed by master sculptor Phidias and built on the site of an earlier temple, the Parthenon in the sixth century was converted into a Christian basilica dedicated to the Virgin Mary, later becoming the Roman Catholic Cathedral of Athens. It was transformed into a Muslim mosque, during Ottoman rule, in the early 1460s. In his revealing book *The Christian Parthenon* (2009) Professor Anthony Kaldellis describes how the city progressed from a university town of the Roman Empire to an important Christian pilgrimage centre.

Although written sources on the Byzantine churches of Athens are scarce, we know that in the eleventh century the Byzantine Emperor Basil II visited the Parthenon to thank the Virgin for his victories. His imperial cortège with all its finery made its way to the Parthenon and endowed it with luxurious gifts, which included a swinging golden dove and burning lamps above the altar. Michael Choniates, Archbishop of Athens, in 1175 delivered his inaugural address here, where he referred repeatedly to the divine light of the temple which illuminated all Attica[1]. With the arrival of the Crusades and ransacking of the temple in 1204, Choniates was replaced by a French archbishop when the Parthenon was converted to a Catholic church.

We pass the base of Phidias' once towering bronze statue of Athena Promachos, defender of the city, literally, 'Athena who fights in the front line', which stood between the Propylaia and the Parthenon. Holding a shield in one hand and a spear in the other, the nine-metre-high, helmeted goddess stood on this spot for over a thousand years overlooking the city. Reflection from the spear's tip was apparently spotted by sailors as they approached Athens from around the Bay of Sounion, 70 kilometres away.

Following the processional route of the annual Panathenaea, we make our way towards the temple, her luminous marble columns reflecting the morning sun. Seemingly straight, in reality irregular and curved, they stand erect against blue sky. We come to the west end, main entrance to the Christian church, where Christian paintings once adorned the walls. Just inside the now closed-off west entrance has survived one of the earliest examples of mid-Byzantine decoration, a style evolved in the Eastern Roman Empire following partition of the old empire by Constantine the Great. The interiors of these tall walls were adorned with paintings, of which only a few sketches survive: an original design of the apse mosaic of the Virgin and Child with two Saints can be seen just inside the west entrance. Also evident are several hundred Christian graffiti, invocations of the faithful addressed to Christ or the Virgin. Just inside on the right of the remains are the lower remnants of a Turkish minaret. Visitors approaching the columned entrance from the Propylaia would have faced a patchwork of colour.

Passing along the Sacred Way, we look up towards the metopes, relief carvings of mythological battles, craning our necks for traces of the long-gone Parthenon frieze. Removed in the early nineteenth century by Lord Elgin's agents, and displayed in the Acropolis and British Museums, the scenes depict Athenian citizens carrying Athena's newly-woven outer robe, or peplos, in the Panathenaic procession. Representing Athenian life in the Classical period, the frieze displays the Greek gift of portraying the beauty of everyday Greek life and legend. Gilded and brightly painted, the finely carved reliefs of jewelled Athenian citizens and sacrificial animals in procession are picked out in detail, revealing coloured headbands and folds of garments with metal and gold fastenings.

We continue along the route, once bedecked with ancient statues and votive offerings, towards the temple entrance at the far (east) end, where the pediment was filled with ancient sculpture displaying the birth of Athena. On the architrave below, can be seen the holes used for displaying spoils of victory, dedicated by Alexander the Great in the later fourth century BC to Athena. Smaller holes on the same façade indicate fixtures used for a bronze-lettering inscription honouring Emperor Nero when he visited Athens in the first century AD. Below, the cella, containing the 12-metre-high gold and ivory statue of Phidias' Parthenon Athena, stood in the shadowed light of the rising sun. A Roman copy of the sculpture in the Athens National Museum, although reduced in size, conveys the grandeur of the original. The Byzantines converted the roofed space of the cella into three naves by two rows of columns and closed off the area with an apse; the roof was opened and the central nave covered by a dome. Frescoes covered the walls and the apse above was adorned with a mosaic of Our Lady of Athens holding the infant Jesus.

In his interesting book *Journey into Greece* (1682), George Wheler, travelling through Athens in 1675, refers to the apse mosaic of the Virgin, apparently left untouched by the Ottoman Turks as, one having done so, suffered a withered hand. Greek Byzantine artists, skilled at blending shades and tints to maximise light, related interior decoration to both natural light and positions of lamps and candles within the building. How, in the curves of the apse, the tesserae would have reflected light streaming through the openings of the eastern doors. How they would have shone in the evening glow of candlelight.

A maze of colour, washed away by the passage of time, the Parthenon overawed medieval travellers, many of whom record seeing an icon of the Virgin, said to have been painted by St Luke. An Italian traveller, Niccolò da Martoni, visiting Athens in 1395, marvelled at the vastness of the 'cathedral' of the Parthenon. He described the magnificent canopy around the altar as being supported on four columns of jasper[2]. Cyriacus of Ancona, Italian antiquarian and papal diplomat, visited the Parthenon in 1436. Overcome by its architectural beauty, he left detailed drawings of the temple as it was then before the Venetian bombardment.[3] The world-traveller Evliya Chelebi, visiting the Acropolis in 1668 during Ottoman rule, wrote of the unimaginable wonders that he had seen in Athens. Enthusing over the two-storey 'mosque' of the Parthenon and its courtyard, he described 300 castle-like houses with balconies. He mentioned statues which seemed to be alive and described piers and columns of red and emerald porphyry carved with brilliant flowers. He saw Plato's marble throne and described slabs of marble which turned red and lit up the interior as the sun rose[4].

A few metres away, in front of the east end of the temple, lies the circular base of a small round temple erected here in 27 BC by the Athenians to the goddess of Rome and Emperor Augustus. This conical structure, vestige of the Roman imperial cult, was partly modelled on the nearby Erechtheion temple, focus of the Panathenaea and religious centre of the Acropolis.

~~~

Looking down from the columns of the Parthenon across the Athenian Plain, we gaze at the timeless landscape of Greece, towards the high peak of Lykabettos and sculptured mountains beyond. In the distance crests the glistening sea and the island of Salamis; further still lies Aegina, its clear, mountainous line visible on the distant horizon. Towards our right (the east) rise the marbled slopes of Mount Penteli and, way off to the north, Mount Parnitha, shimmering in the ethereal light of Greece.

Continuing round the periphery, we come to the Belvedere Terrace, laid out in the nineteenth century for the royal family and which looks out over central Athens. Down below stretches the sanctuary and theatre of Dionysos, origin of dramatic entertainment and European drama. Further round the citadel sits the Erechtheion, started in 420 BC, and last temple on the citadel to be built under Pericles, at the height of the Peloponnesian War, in honour of legendary King Erechtheos. Situated on the northern edge of the rock, the temple housed several shrines and porticos on different ground levels, including a Roman copy of the Parthenon Athena, now in the National Museum. The building was transformed into a two-storey Christian church by converting the eastern porch into a Byzantine apse, removing the pediment, and creating an internal nave and side aisles. Dedicated to the Virgin, it later served as a Catholic bishops' palace for the dukes of Athens, and later still, under the Ottomans, as a residence of the Turkish governor.

In front of this temple, worship of Athena and Poseidon the sea god originated; legend holds that it was here that the contest for patronage of Athens between Athena and Poseidon took place, Athena winning by producing the olive tree, provider of oil, food and timber. Inside the temple stood an olive wood statue of the goddess, said to have fallen from heaven. A sacred snake, which survived on gifts of honey cakes and thought to be the spirit of

Cecrops, half man, half serpent and mythical founder of the city, guarded the temple.

Making our way along the rough path towards the north portico, we stop to marvel, as Emperors Augustus and Hadrian had done, at the Caryatid Porch, or Porch of the Maidens, on the south side, five of the six original maidens, korai, now in the Acropolis Museum, and one in the British Museum. Augustus, admiring this porch, funded its restoration and plaster casts of the Caryatids can be seen in the portico of the Augustan Forum and in the Pantheon, in Rome. Likewise, copies of the Caryatids surround the pool of the Villa Tivoli, Emperor Hadrian's retreat outside the city. How could these marble maidens seemingly stand with such poise, supporting the roof of the south porch? Female figures, each one draped in a peplos pinned at the shoulder and falling in smooth folds, stand serenely. Each replica, crafted individually, reveals the sculptor's artistry in depicting transparent folds of clothing, and intricate hairstyles of thick-braided hair falling down the back into a thick plait.

We make our way round to the north porch, its six Ionic columns contrasting delicately with the thicker Doric columns of the Parthenon. The capitals, once painted with gold leaf, would have been resplendent. Restoration work on the Acropolis has revealed scattered traces of the rare pigment, Egyptian blue, on the coffered ceiling of the temple. Looking up, we can just see the opening supposedly left by the passage of Poseidon's trident when it struck the Acropolis. On looking down at the paving below, we are shown marks commonly believed to have been left by a thunderbolt.

From the edge of the rock, we look down over the North slope of the Acropolis where, hollowed out of the steep rock, invisible from here, lie the rustic shrines of minor deities and the site of the ancient Klepsydra Spring House, once connected to the Erechtheion by a secret staircase. We look further down on the Agora below, at the distant Byzantine churches, terracotta rooftops and alleyways of Plaka. Beyond can be seen the outlines of skyscrapers, satellite dishes and blue sun blinds over the balconies of the modern city. Towards our left lie the hills of Peristeri and Aigaleo, from where King Xerxes, seated on his throne, watched the fall of his naval fleet in the straits of Salamis. Further away rises the bare peak of Lykabettos, crowned with the nineteenth-century, whitewashed chapel of St George.

We turn round towards the Temple of Athena Nike, goddess of victory, facing Piraeus with a view over the sea and Salamis. An eternal figure of Classical beauty, Nike was closely identified with goddess Athena. Built during the Peloponnesian Wars, the temple with her Ionic columns expressed the city's ambition to conquer its longstanding enemy Sparta, and become the main city-state. Designed by Kallikrates in 435 BC on the site of an earlier temple, the cella contained a wooden statue of the goddess holding a branch of pomegranate, symbol of peace. The parapet was decorated with a frieze depicting victory sculptures, which ran parallel with the Propylaia stairway and is now displayed in the Acropolis Museum. Admired by medieval travellers, the small temple with its elegant columns, stood untouched until the Ottoman rulers dismantled it in the seventeenth century to re-use its marble blocks in the construction of fortification walls. After independence the huge slabs of marble were excavated by archaeologists and Athena Nike was restored to its original state.

Leaving the Rock by the Propylaia, we look back and wonder at the curves of the Acropolis, symbol of the Greek nation, and its magnificent desolation. Making our way slowly back down the North slope, past the nymph sanctuary and Klepsydra spring house, we pass the sacred shrines and cave sanctuaries of Pan and other deities. Worship of Pan the shepherd god had developed in Attica after the 490 BC Greek victory at Marathon, believed to have been brought about by intervention of the god. Vital spirits of nature, these demigods and natural deities of trees, springs and hills, known for their prophetic power and healing abilities, played an important role in the daily lives of citizens and those from rural areas.

How exquisitely the architecture blends with the rough landscape. What harmony and balance. The ancient Greeks' search for eternal truth had been a groping towards the light of faith. St John Chrysostom, reading his Paschal sermon in the fourth century, reassured his followers that God did honour the intention. But for apostle Paul in the first century, espying countless pagan statues throughout the city, they were the embodiment of evil.

~~~

The Acropolis Museum

Finally we follow the path down the pedestrian way to the Acropolis Museum. This particular site on Dionysiou Areopagitou was chosen to enable the visitor to experience a close bond with the Parthenon. With a direct view of the temple above, we walk along a glass walkway, below which lie the ruins of part-Roman and early Byzantine settlements, uncovered during the construction of the museum and incorporated into the structure. Built on concrete and steel stilts to withstand a 10 Richter earthquake, the museum is made up of transparent glass floors and walls which filter the Athenian light. The owl, symbol of Athena's wisdom, perches at the entrance where a wondrous world opens out before us.

In the main hall are displayed finds from the sanctuaries and settlements of the North and South slopes of the Acropolis. At the foot of the glass ramp two winged terracotta statues of Nike stand on tall pedestals. Displayed above is part of the long pediment of a sixth-century earlier temple dedicated to Athena, depicting a multicoloured, winged three-bodied monster representing fire, water and air. Known as 'Bluebeard', the sculpture was vividly painted with blue and red tails, and the right-hand head had a blue moustache and beard. On the left of the pediment Herakles, son of Zeus, wrestles with Triton. Slightly higher up, on a balcony overlooking the hall, stand the five freestanding Caryatids from the Erechtheion.

We walk up the glass ramp to the Archaic Gallery, an exhibition of sculpture from the seventh century BC to the end of the Persian Wars. Exhibits comprise the Acropolis

Kores, sculptured sixth-century BC kouroi – life-size, idealised figures of athletic youths and maidens, votive offerings to Athena set up on the Acropolis. Warmed and bathed in sunlight, they stand rigidly, reminiscent of Egyptian statuary. Commissioned by noble, Athenian families and offered as dedications to Apollo and other gods, the kouroi were commonly used as grave markers and commemorative statues for winners in the ancient Games. Buried by the Athenians after the 480 BC Persian sack of the Acropolis, they were discovered by archaeologists in the nineteenth century, amongst debris.

The kouroi and korai, representing the great awakening of Greek sculpture in the seventh century BC, are unique for their grace and naturalness, and the characteristic 'archaic smile'. They embody restraint, dignity and harmony - pervaded by a vital spirit. Not to be missed are: the Acropolis Sphinx; the Calf-Bearer, representing a man bearing a sacrificial calf; sixth-century BC horse-riders, notably, the Rampin Horseman dedicated to Athena; the sweetly-smiling maidens, Peplos Kore, wearing a green necklace and radiant in a faintly coloured, decorated peplos, and the Maiden of Chios; and the fifth-century BC Kritian Boy, described by Kenneth Clark in his book *The Nude: A Study of Ideal Art* (1960) as the first beautiful nude in art. What poise. What energy. His toned, athletic physique encapsulates the essence of ancient Greek belief that a healthy mind and body, a combined athletic moral training, was essential for the success of the democratic ideal. Noteworthy too is the fifth-century BC plaque representing Mourning Athena with a Corinthian helmet, and the fourth-century BC idealised Head of the Young

Alexander the Great, one of the greatest conquerors the world has ever known.

On the top floor, the Parthenon Gallery, a replica of the actual Parthenon, contains a glass rotating platform displaying the Parthenon frieze and overlooking the modern city. From the platform we view the sculpture and look up to the temple, at the same time placing the marbles of the frieze, metopes and pediments in their original position alongside copies of those in the British Museum. Through the glass floor we see down to the underground excavations of ancient Athens, thus linking the foundations of the old town to the Parthenon and the modern city.

On our way back down to the first floor, we pause to look at the Erechtheion frieze, the freestanding Caryatids, and battle scenes from the Athena Nike Temple. Of particular note is the headless but timeless Nike Adjusting her Sandal, from the temple parapet. Here, the simplicity and nobility of Classical art at the end of the century, at around 410 BC, are seen in the depiction of loose folds of transparent, swaying drapery indicating slight movement, clinging to the goddess's body, suggesting the contours underneath.

After viewing exhibits from early Christian and Roman Athens, we leave the Acropolis behind. Emerging into bright sunshine on Dionysiou Areopagitou, we escape the fever of the European capital for the coastal road and Glyfada, for a long-awaited swim.

4. Ancient Agora and the Temple of Hephaistos, God of Fire

Further along Apostolou Pavlou, past the Areopagus, we turn right into a wooded path towards the Hephaisteion, temple of Hephaistos, god of metallurgy and craftsmen. The structure is dedicated to the god and his sister Athena, goddess of the Arts, both patrons of artisans. Part of Pericles' plan to rebuild Athens after the Persian wars, the Hephaisteion was started in the mid-fifth century BC at about the same time as construction began on the Parthenon. With its slender honey-coloured columns, the temple emerges unexpectedly from behind pines. It sits stoically but self-effacingly on the low Kolonos Hill which was, in antiquity, a meeting place for Athenian craftsmen. Made from Pentelic marble, the Hephaisteion, of incomparable beauty, is one of the best preserved temples in Greece, its peristyle of thirty-four columns intact.

According to one story, son of Zeus and Hera, Hephaistos was born lame and hurled down from Mount Olympus into the sea, from where he was rescued by nymphs. Passing his time on the seabed collecting coral and pearl, he fashioned jewellery for his rescuers. To gain revenge for his ill-treatment, he made a magic throne which was sent to Olympus and presented to the goddess to entrap her. Refusing to return to the mountain to set her free, the god was intoxicated by Dionysos and returned to the mountain. Hera was only released when Hephaistos was granted delightful, goddess Aphrodite as a bride.

With its golden-brown patina, the temple exudes warmth, its sun-beaten Doric columns rising against blue sky. Where once noise from local metalworkers echoed through the temple's columns, silence prevails now, broken only by the cicada song, clicking of digital cameras, and the occasional, raised voice of a distant guide. To our right (the south) rises the Areopagus and beyond, the Acropolis. Overlooking the ruins of the Agora and surrounded by a sacred grove of trees, the Hephaisteion was watered by a stream from the Pnyx. Sculptured friezes towards the east end, depicting scenes of the Labours of Heracles, exploits of the hero Theseus and the Battles of the Centaurs, *remain intact.* Colossal bronze statues of the two gods, both revered in antiquity and praised by Roman writers Pausanius and Cicero once dominated the interior.

In the seventh century the temple, which was outside the city wall, was converted into the church of St George, patron saint of Greece. An entrance was constructed in the west end and an apse was constructed in the east by removing two columns and installing an arch and a new barrel-vaulted roof. Survivor of earthquakes and invasions (marked by bullet holes), the Hephaisteion was saved from demolition and conversion into a mosque on the orders of the sultan: its doors were to be opened for the liturgy once a year only, giving it the nickname 'The Idler'. The surrounding area was used as a Christian burial ground until the 1830s and in 1834 a church service was held here to welcome the new king and queen to Athens.

From the east terrace we look down over the ruins of the ancient Agora, nucleus of Athenian government and democratic life. Commercial and administrative centre of ancient Athens, the marketplace was the hub and soul of the city, where all roads in and out of the city met. Amongst the shrines to their Gods, and statues of generals and tyrant killers, Athenians gathered in the Agora to exchange news, do business and legislate. Here walked brilliant men: architects and sculptors, historians and inventors of dramatic poetry; explorers of mathematics, medicine and astronomy, and inventors of the astronomical computer; men who gave us democracy, philosophy and politics, and more. Within sight of the Parthenon, Athenians, reassured by the presence of their goddess, questioned old traditions, searching for an understanding of Man and his place in the scheme of created things (the meaning of our lives), setting the foundation for Western thought and culture.

Devastated by invasions in the third century AD, followed by the closure of the philosophical schools and further invasions in the sixth century, destruction and rebuilding in the Agora continued on and off until the nineteenth century. The site was taken over in the 1930s by the American School of Classical Studies, when some four hundred residences were removed to allow excavations.

Below lie the ruined state buildings of the ancient city, a sacred precinct. Directly to our left, near the railway line, lie fragments of the Stoa of Zeus, a shaded meeting place where Socrates walked with his pupils. Here, Pausanius tells us, paintings of battles, dedicated to the God in thanksgiving for Greek victories, adorned the walls. Beyond the Stoa in the northwest corner lie the ruins of the small Stoa Basileus, or Royal Stoa, the office of the chief archon, which displayed the ancient laws of the city on its walls. It was here that the philosopher was formally charged with impiety. Further over to the left, on the north side of the Agora, lie the ruins of the Stoa Poikile, or Painted Porch, where in the early third century BC, the first Stoic School of Philosophy was founded, its walls adorned with captured bronze shields and paintings of Greek victories at Troy and Marathon.

To the right of the Stoa of Zeus, directly in front of us, lie the foundations of the late Classical temple of Apollo Patroos, which held a colossal statue of Apollo the lyre player, now in the Agora Museum. Further to our right lie the remains of the Metroon, a second-century BC sanctuary of the Mother of the Gods, which housed the state archives. Just above the Metroon, built into the hillside, are the remains of the fifth-century BC New Bouleuterion, or Council House, meeting place of the

Senate. The round base of the mid-fifth-century BC Tholos, headquarters of the Council of 500 (Boule), lies lower down. And further to the right of the Tholos can be seen the remains of what is recognised as Simon the Cobbler's workshop, frequented by Socrates and his friends. Directly to our right, next to the south-west fountain-house, lie the ruined Heliaia, the sixth-century BC Supreme law courts of Athens, where the philosopher was tried in 399 BC.

At the far (east) end of the Agora stands the Agora Museum, the rebuilt two-storied Hellenistic Stoa of Attalus, a gallery of shops and promenades, from where the people of Athens could watch the Panathenaic procession.

~~~

Here in the Agora sprang visible signs of the expanding Roman Empire: in the centre of the market place, near the altar of Zeus Agoraios, stood the second-century BC 1000-seater Odeion, a roofed concert hall built by General Agrippa, son-in-law of Emperor Augustus. Close by was the relocated ancient Temple of Ares, god of war, identified with Gaius, the 'New Ares' and grandson of Augustus, next to a bronze statue of Demosthenes, the greatest of Greek orators. In the near distance stands a headless statue of Emperor Hadrian, his upper torso just visible above the trees. His body armour depicts Greek goddess Athena standing on a she-wolf feeding Romulus and Remus, founders of Rome - Greece dominating Rome while being dominated by her. Close by, tower the heads of the sculptured Giants and Tritons of the burnt-out

Odeion, re-used for the colonnaded entrance of the fifth-century Gymnasium, the new university.

Down to our right, in the far corner, stands the mid-Byzantine church of the Holy Apostles (Ayii Apostoli); beyond, the Areopagus and further still, the Acropolis. Nearer, next to the Stoa of Attalos sit the ruins of the Pantainos Library, a public building erected in the second century AD on the road to the Roman Forum. Dedicated to Athena Polis, protector of the city, and Emperor Trajan, it faced the Panathenaic Way. An inscription on the wall displays the longstanding library rule that no books were to be removed from the centre. Over all, in the stillness, can be heard the distant, hourly peal of the church of St Philip where, legend holds, the apostle held his sermons.

Deserted after third-century raids, the administrative centre was moved to the nearby Roman Forum. Invasions continued into the sixth century, but Christianity was making inroads within the empire. The museum displays artefacts from the Neolithic era through the Roman and Byzantine periods. Alongside statuary and everyday items, noteworthy exhibits include: an Archaic oil-flask of a kneeling athlete binding a ribbon; a fifth-century BC water-clock used for timing speeches in court cases; inscribed pottery fragments used in voting to ostracise politicians; a fourth-century BC decree of Athenian Law for Democracy, depicting Democracy crowning the people of Athens; a Hellenistic marble device used for electing citizens to public offices; and early Christian lamps inscribed with the *chi-rho* sign, symbol of Constantine's new Christian Empire.

~~~

We clamber down a rough path through the ancient site towards Holy Apostles Church, sole surviving Byzantine church of nine in the Agora. In the debris, broken Hellenistic columns lie strewn alongside fragmented statue bases. Built around the remains of a Roman fountain-house and the ruined fifth-century BC Athenian Mint, the church was dedicated to the Seventy Apostles.

The Holy Apostles is one of many churches founded by the local aristocracy during the tenth to twelfth centuries when, at a time of increasing prosperity, Byzantines were building and exterior decoration was flourishing. The iconoclastic controversy, destruction of religious images, had been finally resolved and icon worship restored to the Eastern Orthodox Church, in 843, by Empress Theodora, widow of Emperor Theophilus. The Byzantines had recaptured Crete from the Arabs in 961; Emperor Basil, in 1019, successfully conquered the Bulgars and prayed at the church of the Holy Virgin in the Parthenon; and Athens had become an archbishop's see. Having survived burning and attacks in the Agora by Franks, Turks and Venetians, the church was restored to its original state in the mid-1950s by the American School.

Isolated amongst the ruins of the Agora, the church stands out with its stone and brick decoration, an architectural style developed in Constantinople in the fifth century and adopted by the Byzantines. The central-planned, flat-roofed, traditional Roman basilica had been transformed into a four-armed, central cross-in-square plan, topped by a dome, a traditional Eastern feature. Typical characteristics of the Athenian churches of this period are fine brickwork, red-tiled octagonal domes with double-light windows and arched cornices. Marble door frames, window colonettes and floors of marble inlay in the style of churches of Constantinople, were frequently seen. Frescoes and wall mosaics featuring scenes from the life of Christ, lit by narrow windows in the dome, adorned the walls. Following the style of the St Sophia in Constantinople, the interiors were adorned with polychromatic marble. Symmetry and a feeling of movement, symmetry, irradiated by the rhythmic flow of life, underpins all Byzantine art.

A tall dome representing the vaults of heaven, set on a drum pierced with arched double-light windows, rises above triangular gable roofs. We wander round the church to the west entrance, where decorated arched niches representing the Holy Trinity crown three doors. Small windows, creating an impression of invisible light radiating from within, are framed by Eastern style arches and crowned by dogtooth ornament. Decorated brickwork on the upper reaches of the building creates a subtly coloured effect. Embedded in the walls are simply carved ornamental bands and ceramic plaques with letters imitating old Arabic script, an innovation inspired at the time by contact with Arabs. The interior would have contained fine, sculptural ornamentation, of which a restored marble floor and altar remain. Four large and four small half-domes rise to the level of the main dome, which rests on four marble columns, imparting a feeling of harmony and space.

Here, in this rugged corner of the ancient Agora, sits a unique example of Christian fervour, of a world power which lasted nearly a thousand years and which, in 555 under Justinian 1, spanned Europe, Asia and Africa. Finely decorated by unknown artists, stylised but unpretentious, the Holy Apostles Church encapsulates the spirituality of the mid-Byzantine era (843-1204), when worship of icons had been restored in Byzantium and Greek culture again shone in a dark world.

~~~

Exiting the Agora, we make our way towards the ancient cemetery of Kerameikos, pausing to visit the small chapel of Incorporeal Saints (Ayii Assomati) on Assomati Square. Past industrial units and local shops of this former working people's neighbourhood, we reach the church, a solitary building with purple bougainvillea growing up the brickwork and silver-green olive leaves entwined with orange trees. The decorated stone recalls that of the Holy Apostles and is characteristic of the cruciform, Athenian churches of this period. Incorporated into the façade are two terracotta plaques with ornaments and old Arabic lettering, and above the northern entrance sits a horseshoe arch, indicating Islamic influence.

A young Greek woman sitting outside the church, curiously watching us as we photograph the colours, strikes up a conversation in half Greek and broken English, claiming that the lushness of the plants derives from the dry soil of Athens, where Athena's sacred olive flourished. 'The soil!' she exclaims, proud of her country's heritage whilst enquiring if we are British or American.

Where did I learn Greek? Are we visiting Athens alone? Have we visited the islands yet? Do I find Athens has changed? Yes, Greece is very beautiful, our friend agrees, adding that she works in Germany and has come home to celebrate Easter. Reminding us that the country *has* changed a lot, she talks about politicians, migrants, World War II and the current financial meltdown, before enthusing over the delights of her native Greek cooking at Easter time. Then, guessing that we might be feeling somewhat peckish, our friend, her eyes lighting up, points us in the direction of Athens Central Market to experience first-hand, fresh Greek fish and vegetables.

A short distance away, in the old potters' quarter of the city, lies the half-ruined, ancient cemetery of Kerameikos, behind the city's ancient walls. Used as a burial site until the fourth or fifth century, Kerameikos was reserved for the rich and those citizens, particularly male, of social rank. Here, at the ancient Sacred and Dipylon Gates, converged three roads, lined with tombs and statues of statesmen: one road led south to Piraeus, another northwards to Plato's Academy and the third westwards to Eleusis and Corinth.

The Sacred Gate, starting point of the Eleusinian procession, was topped with a marble sphinx. Dipylon, the largest gate in ancient Greece, was the starting point of the Panathenaic Procession and cavalry escort, from where all participants set out along the Holy Way, crossed the Agora and climbed to the Acropolis. Between the two gateways, stands the ruined Pompeion, preparation area for the festival processions, the paved floor of these areas still displaying ruts cut by passing chariot wheels. It was in front of this gateway that Pericles delivered his Funeral Oration, glorifying democracy and honouring those who had died in the Peloponnesian War.

Branching off to our left southwards is the ancient Street of the Tombs. The faint murmuring of a stream reminds us that this was and remains an area of natural beauty. Covered over but visible here, the ancient Eridanos trickles, its tang permeating the mid-afternoon air. A vital source of fresh water in antiquity, the small river flowed down from Lycabettos through the city out towards the Saronic Gulf. Surviving funerary monuments and sarcophagi, scattered amongst pomegranate and orange trees, laurels and palms, revive treasured moments of times past, suggesting the splendid lives of those, in bygone days, who loved living.

We pass replicas of Young Dexileos on Horseback, and a marble bull, symbol of strength and fertility, raised over the tomb of a rich treasurer, and opposite, the family grave stele of Hegeso. Exhibits inside the nearby museum include sculpture from the Archaic, Classical, Hellenistic and Roman periods. Notable artefacts include a sixth-century marble sphinx; a grave relief of Dexileos; children's graves; funerary vases; and pottery dedicated to victims of the Athens plague.

Leaving Kerameikos behind, as shadows lengthen over the Eridanos, we set off, hungry, towards Ermou and Monastiraki to find a traditional Greek taverna. Turning a corner, we come upon an old square with a splashing fountain and pavements covered with tables and humming with activity. People sit chatting over ouzo or a light beer and ice, others sit sipping Greek coffee. In the late afternoon light the city breathes fresh life but, too early to eat, we find an old ouzerie where we relax under a plane tree, returning to eat later in the evening with friends.

5. Roman Forum, Hadrian's Library, Monastiraki and Zorba's Dance

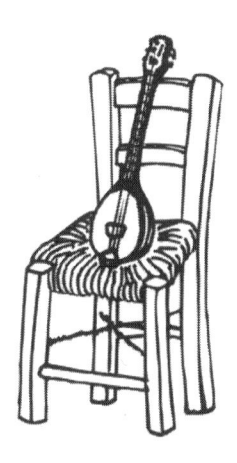

A short stroll away from the church of the Holy Apostles in the Agora and behind the street markets of Monastiraki, stands the Athena Archegetis gateway, monumental western entrance of the Roman Forum. Financed by both Julius Caesar and Augustus, the arch reflects the confidence of the post-Hellenistic age, when Romans were building and restoring monuments in Athens, a city of religious, intellectual and artistic prestige.

Situated in the centre of the town, the rectangular forum became the trading centre of oil production and the main market of Athens, until it was destroyed by fire in 1884. Dedicated by the Athenians to their patroness, it was later connected to the Stoa of Attalos in the Agora by a colonnaded street of marble, reached by monumental stairways. Built in the later part of the first century BC, stretching up to the Tower of the Winds and Hadrian's Library, the Roman forum functioned as a commercial and administrative centre until the late nineteenth century, when excavations began. Four Ionic columns of Hymettan marble survive of a smaller entrance close to a series of shops and public latrines at the far (east) end.

The four surviving Doric columns of the western arched gateway hint at the majesty and grandeur of the original entrance, built in Pentelic marble in the form of a Doric temple façade. Symbol of early Roman imperialism, the arch was surmounted by an equestrian statue of Augustus' adopted son and heir, Lucius, dedicated by the Athenians after the boy's death in AD 2. A worn inscription on the architrave of the façade reveals the building was dedicated to Athena Archegetis (Leader), due to the generosity of both Caesar and Augustus. On the north side of the doorway, facing the Acropolis, is an engraving of Hadrian's Athenian oil law, regulating the sale of oil and excise duty, whereby olive growers had to deliver one third of their olive oil to Athens.

During the Ottoman years, when the forum was used as a wheat market, a Byzantine church, Our Lady of the Market Gate (Ayia Sotira Pazaroportas), stood against this gateway, near a water fountain. In what was a highly populated area of prominent Athenian families, another portico stood on the right (south) side of the forum, where shaded stoa housed shops around another fountain, the daily meeting-place of local women.

Within sight of the western gateway in Dexippou Street,

sits the nineteenth-century church of the Archangels, replacing a small twelfth-century Byzantine chapel. Inside this church is housed a miraculous icon of the Virgin Mary, known as the *Grigorousa*. Every Saturday evening, outside the entrance, a stone's throw from the gateway of the forum, spiced raison and cinnamon *fanouropita* bread is traditionally blessed and distributed to local people. Named after St Fanourios, patron saint of missing objects, the blessed cakes are believed to help people find what is lost, both material and spiritual.

The gateway to the forum opens on to a marble-pillared courtyard. Scarred by time, seemingly untouched by restoration, the blue-grey colonnades of Hymettan marble convey the former splendour of this long-abandoned people's market. Scattered slabs of marble paving installed by Emperor Hadrian remain in place. A residential area in Byzantine and post-Byzantine periods, signs of two demolished Byzantine churches speak of a once densely populated community. Early nineteenth-century artist-travellers' paintings and engravings of the area and its churches, displayed in the Museum of the City of Athens, nostalgically depict these now-vanished landscapes.

Reaching the Fethiye Mosque, built to commemorate the visit of Sultan Mehmet II to Athens in 1458, we stroll round the truncated columns of what was a mid-Byzantine, three-aisle basilica and which had, during the Frankish era, served as the cathedral of Athens. Panels of the church are incorporated into the mosque walls. Broken tomb stones and carved Christian stonework of fragmented, marble slabs incised with Christian crosses lie scattered. Known as the 'Wheatmarket Mosque' during Ottoman rule, the arcaded entrance stands near the lower steps of a now destroyed Turkish minaret. During the Venetian, six-month siege of Athens in the seventeenth century, the building was used as a Catholic church.

Beyond the mosque sit the foundations of a 68-seater public latrine round a large, paved area. Popular places of socialising, multiseat latrines were widespread throughout the Roman world. Close by stands the Agoranomeion, a triple-ached entrance to what may have been a temple dedicated to an emperor. A ruined gate on a corner across the road is all that remains of one of the few Turkish monuments left in Athens, the Medresse, or Turkish seminary.

In front of us stands the Tower of the Winds, an octagonal, hydraulic clock of marble, around which the Romans built their market, referred to by Evliya Chelebi as a gathering place of distinguished men. Designed by an astronomer in the first century BC and powered by the Klepsydra spring on the Acropolis, it is perhaps the oldest surviving weather vane in history. In Byzantine times the tower was used as a church and surrounded by a cemetery. Set on a three-stepped base near the eastern gateway, ornamental friezes bear reliefs of personifications of wind deities, whose apparent simplicity of line and elegance belie an intricacy of workmanship. Beneath these figures eight faded sundials have survived. The weather vane, once topped with a revolving, bronze Triton, pointed to the prevailing wind, crucial information for merchants awaiting shipments. A sea god and son of Poseidon, Triton, half man, half fish, would blow on a shell to raise or calm the waves. It is said that a world mirror, like that of the Pharos Lighthouse of Alexandria, was set on the stylus of the tower, in which enemies approaching from any direction were revealed.

~~~

Just west of the forum, off Monastiraki and what was the old Turkish bazaar, sit the foundations of the once great library of Emperor Hadrian. Modelled on a Roman forum, this massive, rectangular complex and administrative centre comprised a cloistered Corinthian arcade round a pool and garden, adorned with large statues of Athena and Hadrian. Restored after the invasions of 267 and probably the most sumptuous Roman building in Athens at the time, it housed the city's tax archives and philosophical schools until the schools were closed down in 529. Its central courtyard consisted of a large early Byzantine church, probably founded by Empress Eudoxia, Christian wife of Emperor Theodosius II. Destroyed during the invasions of 582, the church was replaced in the eleventh century by the Great Church of Our Lady (Megali Panayia).

A row of massive Corinthian columns dominates the western entrance of the library. A few surviving, veined marble pilasters of the portico hint at the bygone magnificence of this huge, marble complex. On the walls are traces of a sixteenth-century fresco of the Last Judgement, all that remains of a twelfth-century private chapel, Archangels on the Steps (Ayios Assomatos sta Skalia). Finds from the tombs of this little church can be viewed in the small Victoria Romana Museum on the library site. How charming this tiny, domed chapel would have looked, set on what was then a narrow stepped street, niched up against the imposing Corinthian colonnade of Hadrian's Library.

We enter the vast, interior courtyard, originally enclosed by 100 multiveined Corinthian columns. An unfurling expanse of ruined pilasters and architectural fragments, once decorated with gilded roofwork and alabaster, stretches to the far wall where the now-vacant niches housed the ancient rolls of papyrus. In the larger, central recess stood a tall statue of Athena, goddess of wisdom. In the middle of the courtyard stand four remaining columns of the single-aisle, eleventh-century domed church and first cathedral of the city, Megali Panayia, where, it is said, an icon painted of Mary, supposedly by St Luke, was kept. Built over the remains of a fifth-century basilica in what was the heart of the administrative centre of Athens, fragments of a mosaic floor and foundations can still be seen.

In the far corner of the courtyard, not far from the rows of shelving, lie the ruins of a small, three-aisle chapel built during the Frankish occupation and gutted by the 1884 fire.

~~~

We leave the Roman world for the oriental atmosphere and street sounds of the commercialised and now pedestrianised square of Monastiraki (Little Monastery), centre of Byzantine and Ottoman Athens. Opposite the library on Areos street, Turkish-type market shops with rows of brightly coloured shoes and leathered sandals hang down over makeshift doorways. Nearby, iron railings all but hide a little courtyard with a picturesque post-Byzantine church, that of St Elissaios. Built as a private chapel during Ottoman rule, inexplicably demolished in 1943, it was restored to its original state in 2004. A cheerful *philakas,* or guardian, allows us inside the minute single-aisle chapel, frequented at the end of the nineteenth century by the reclusive writer, Alexandros Papadiamantis, and parish priest, Papa Nicholas Planas. Dimly lit and simply furnished, icons of the much loved saint, known as the simple shepherd and who in the nineteenth century served as priest here, hang in the interior.

Emerging into bright sunshine, we are waylaid by the philakas and his lady companion, who tell us at length about the two spiritual men, before regaling us with the full story of the Parthenon marbles. Raising their voices, they gesture to the far end of a long narrow path, towards a tall dilapidated house which belonged in the early 1800s to the then British Consul, and is said to be where Lord Elgin stored the Parthenon friezes.

This area, known in the Turkish period as the lower bazaar, stretched from the public fountain into Hadrian's Library and around Kapnikarea church. Here, where Athenians throng the square and vendors wind in and out spreading their wares, ancient and modern civilisations meet. Today, Holy Thursday, the most popular merchandise are fireworks and decorated Easter eggs, symbol of the renewal of life. To our right, adjoining the west wall of Hadrian's Library, stands, with its triple-arched portico, the Eastern-style, eighteenth-century Tzisdarakis Mosque, built in the lower bazaar by the Turkish governor on the Acropolis. Raised high above warehouses and shops and reached by a flight of steps, the graceful building, with a flattened Byzantine dome, now serves as the Greek Folk Art Museum. Opposite the mosque stands the nineteenth-century Monastiraki metro station, on the corner of a turning down to Athens flea market.

We pass the offices of Boroume, a food aid charity and soup kitchen catering for the thousands of struggling Athenians during the continuing economic crisis. Behind, a short distance away towards our right, the Acropolis glows in the mid-afternoon sun. Across the square, cradled in the shadows of modern blocks, sits the small, restored basilican church, the Virgin Mary, Queen of All (Pantanassa), venerated by the Byzantines as goddess and patron saint of Athens. In the middle of the square, down through ground-level glass panels, can be seen the excavated river bed of the ancient Eridanos, unearthed in the nineteenth century during building of the Athens metro.

One of the oldest churches in Athens, once linked to Kaisariani monastery on Hymettos, the Pantanassa became part of a large religious community. A sprawling convent dating back to the tenth century, the nuns cared for the poor and earned their keep by weaving cloth for stalls of the surrounding bazaar. Having survived the 1827 uprising, the monastery was pulled down during the metro excavations.

Built to withstand burning sunshine, the church with its thick-walled façade and tiny windows, was at the end of the nineteenth century shorn of its frontal architecture. Bereft, the austere, unadorned basilica belies what was once the finely decorated façade of one of the most important parish churches in Byzantine Athens. Representing a period of transition from late antiquity to the Byzantine world, above the central door a recess, now bare, held a fresco of the Virgin and Child surrounded by saints. Renovated Corinthian capitals of the original façade grace the corners. Restored in 1911, when the bell tower was added, a modern seating wall surrounding the sunken church provides a resting point for the unemployed.

~~~

Somewhat hungry, drawn by the acrid aroma of spices and cheeses, we make our way along Athinas Street towards the central market and Omonia, centre of commercial Athens. Passing stands of multicoloured cloths and carpeting, we come to stalls stacked with shining, succulent fruit and all-coloured vegetables, ranging from small okra to massive aubergines, before reaching the indoor market. Barrels of figs and olives of different shades of black, green and purple, of all sizes, stand near sacks of pulses and piles of strong-smelling cheeses.

Inside the noisy meat arcades, cuts of meat from every

kind of animal on wooden butchers' blocks line the aisles. Wall-to-wall lamb carcasses are strung up in readiness for the Easter celebration. Frenzied men, shouldering joints in plastic bags for their Easter barbecue, rush about through the crowds, bargaining loudly with merchants. Impatient passers-by shout, seize and weigh pigs' feet or skinned sheep's heads in a market where thousands of shoppers pass each day. Above a constant hum of raised voices, traders call out their products and prices.

On through the iced stalls of the sea-fresh, fish hall, we cross the slippery floor, drawn by loud voices and sounds of live *bouzoukia*, the people's music, pouring from an underground tavern. Turning a corner, down steps, we stumble upon a dingy, smoky, rustic-type room where barrels of wine line the walls; a bevy of boisterous locals sit at laden tables, gesticulating, drinking retsina. Amidst a growing atmosphere of *kéfi*, (Greek high spirits), a trio of musicians sing and strum *rebetika* songs - old folk rhythms of yearning and homesickness, introduced into Greece in 1923 by refugees from Asia Minor.

Squeezing into a narrow space and shouting across the table to be heard, we order *avgolemono*, chicken soup with egg-lemon sauce, and *fassolakia*, green beans in tomato sauce, whilst overflowing plates of *horiatiki* topped with black olives and feta, arrive with a carafe of local wine. At the neighbouring table locals raise their glasses to us as a friendly gesture, offering us retsina to try. '*Yiassas*'– 'Your health!' we call, as we pick at the different appetisers. We are urged to join in the spirit, whilst yet another carafe of wine and tumblers of iced water come round.

Soon an older man leaps up from a table and begins to dance the *Zeibekiko*, his slow and driven manner moving with the pounding rhythm of the *bouzouki* strings. One by one, another man gets up to dance, each one rapt, eyes cast downwards, moving in a trance. Our spirits rising as we fall under the spell of the *bouzouki*'s staccato rhythms, we enjoy the mood with our new friends, steadfastly downing our wine, the twanging of *bouzouki* electrifying the smoke-filled room and following us out along the crowded streets.

1: The Acropolis of Athens

2 (above): 'Mask of Agamemnon' from the Greek Bronze Age
3 (below): The Parthenon, opened about 432 BC

4 (above): Porch of Caryatids, Erechtheion, later 5th century BC
5 (below): Reclining Dionysos, Parthenon east pediment

6 (above): Horse Riders in procession, Parthenon frieze
7 (below): Kerameikos, Street of the Tombs

8: Bearer carrying a sacrificial calf, 6th century BC
9: Theatre of Dionysos, Acropolis south slope

10 (above left): Detail of 19th-century statue of Socrates, Athens Academy
11 (above right): Detail of black-figure Attic vase showing Herakles fighting a centaur, 7th century BC
12 (below): View of Mt Lykabettos and St George Chapel

13 (above left): Athenian Owl dekadrachm coin showing the bejewelled goddess wearing an Attic helmet decorated with olive. Symbol of owl shown on reverse

14 (above right): Bust of Emperor Hadrian, National Archaeological Museum, Athens
15 (below): Byzantine church of the Holy Apostles

16 (above): 14th-century Icon of Archangel Michael carrying a sceptre and transparent cross-topped globe
17 (below): Monastiraki Square with mosque

18 (above): View from Odeon of Herodes Atticus, looking
out towards the Aegean
19 (below): A Street in Plaka

20 (above): Louis Spyridon, first modern marathon winner, entering Kallimarmaro Stadium at the 1896 Athens Olympics
21 (below): Changing of the Guard, Parliament Building

6. Hadrian's City, a Greek Orthodox Baptism and Byzantine Museum

Athens' greatest treasure, many Athenians would say, is the National Garden, originally the private park of King Otto and Queen Amalia, situated behind the Greek Parliament. To escape the frenetic pace of the city, we wander through the garden gates into a hushed world where narrow pathways wind round sub-tropical trees. Athenians sit relaxing amongst exotic shrubs or stroll through shaded paths towards the garden café or children's zoo. Designed by Queen Amalia, first Queen of Greece and lover of parks, the National Gardens originally contained over 15,000 flowers and trees from around the world.

In *The Colossus of Maroussi* (1941) Henry Miller wrote that these Gardens remained in his memory like no other park. Modern statuary of celebrated Greek poets and national leaders stand round corners where homeless stretch out on benches amongst fountains and wildlife. Ancient fragments and a mosaic floor from a Roman villa lie hidden near a duck pond. Peacocks strut around a neoclassical pavilion, from where sounds of fun and laughter lead us along secluded, tree-lined paths to a water turtle lake near a small monkey zoo and children's playground.

On leaving this haven, we emerge into the racket of congested six-lane Amalias, beneath yellowing cassia and green fig trees, before reaching the recently discovered Roman baths and Hadrian's Arch at a traffic-filled junction. Revered by both Greeks and Romans, the fig of Attica, so sacred was it held, had in the sixth century BC been banned from export out of Greece. It was rumoured that Xerxes' plans to invade the country had centred around his passion for this fruit. Pink-blossomed Judas trees, efflorescent and in full bloom, line the noisy avenue. As we pass a statue of Lord Byron dying in the arms of Greece, scents of pink oleander cross our path.

~~~

Hadrian's Arch, connecting Emperor Hadrian's new town to ancient Athens, marked an ancient road linking the Acropolis to the Olympeion. The land slopes down from Lykabettos to the riverbed of the sacred Ilissos. The gateway, close to the river, was built by the Athenians in the second century in honour of their emperor. Surrounded by hurtling traffic and wild flowers, the arch consists of two layers - a lower Roman gateway, through which people and animals could pass, crowned by a series of Corinthian columns and a pediment. Through the upper arches of the pediment can be seen the long ridge of Hymettos. Two inscriptions are carved on the architrave of the arch, the Acropolis side reading: 'This is Athens, the ancient city of Theseus'; the second, on the side facing the new city, reads: 'This is the city of Hadrian and not of Theseus'.

Beyond the monumental entrance soar the Corinthian columns of the Olympeion. Situated outside the city, the temple was built on the site of an earlier sanctuary dedicated to Zeus. Set against a backdrop of blue-grey slopes of Hymettos, the remaining 15 columns present a vision of majesty and power. Begun by the Peisistratid tyrants, in the sixth century BC and frequently abandoned, the temple was eventually completed over 600 years later in 131, by Emperor Hadrian, one of the greatest benefactors to the Roman Empire and Athens.

Honoured as a god by Athenians, set to make the city the cultural capital of the empire, Hadrian set up the Panhellenion League, an organisation of Hellenes from Greek city-states across the Greek-speaking world, its purpose being to unite all Greeks reconciled under Roman rule. A huge enclave was installed round the temple within which, perhaps, meetings of the Panhellenios and the annual Panhellenia festival took place. Embellishing the city with aqueducts, a pantheon, a library and a nymphaeum, he extended his new town to the other side of the Ilissos, doubling the size of the city. An ardent admirer of Greek culture, Hadrian encouraged the growth of philosophical schools and revived the sciences. Restoring beauty to the city of Athens at the time of an expanding empire, he revitalised Athenian life.

The Olympeion consisted of 104 columns arranged in double and triple colonnades. It contained a huge gold and ivory statue of Zeus seated on an elaborate throne. Half-draped, the god held a victory in one hand, and a sceptre in the other. The sculpture was modelled on Phidias' statue of Zeus at Olympia, carved in the fifth century BC and considered one of the Seven Wonders of the World. The largest cult statue in antiquity, the giant-seated figure of Zeus stood next to one of Hadrian himself, identified with the Olympeion Zeus. Numerous statues of the emperor, dedicated by Greek cities, were scattered around the forecourt of the temple and throughout the town.

How magnificently carved are the remaining Corinthian capitals, decorated with the Egyptian acanthus motif. What authority. Everlasting symbol of imperial power, in 131 the Olympeion was referred to by the Roman poet Julia Babilla as absolute perfection and beauty, created by power, described by Elizabeth Speller in her interesting book *Following Hadrian* (2004).

By the mid-fifteenth century 80 of the temple's columns had collapsed. Having fallen into disuse over time, the neglected building was eventually used as a church. Italian traveller, Cyriacus of Ancona, in 1436 saw only 21 of the original 104 pilasters. Another column was ground down in 1760 by the Turkish governor, to be used in the construction of the Tsisdarakis mosque in Monastiraki, for which the culprit was eventually punished. Strewn across the ground, the massive drums of another column blown down in a hurricane remain as they fell.

Entering the sanctuary, we pass remaining, ancient city wall and a Roman bath complex, before following the route round the temple that the Roman emperors would have followed. Ahead rises the peak of Lykabettos, crowned with the white chapel of St George, from where at midnight on Easter Sunday, hundreds of Orthodox candle-holding worshippers will wend their way down the slopes into the streets of the town below. Looking back, between the tall office blocks of the modern city, the sheer rock of the Acropolis hovers, whilst before us lies Hymettos. Further on (across the river in Hadrian's time) sits the Stadium in a hollow on the edge of Ardettos Hill and to our left, spreading outwards, the European city.

Walking round behind the temple, on the south side, we look over the Ilissos valley excavation site. Near the river bed ran the fountain of Kalirrhoe, 'pleasantly flowing' spring, which supplied the ancient city with drinking water. It was on the banks of this stream, Plato wrote in *Phaedrus* (370 BC), that Socrates strolled with his pupils and prayed at the cave of Pan, the shepherd god. And legend tells us that from this river-edge, Boreas, Greek god of the north wind, carried off the beautiful maiden, Oreithia, daughter of legendary King Erechtheus, whilst she was gathering flowers.

~~~

Leaving the Olympeion, we walk round the south side towards the nineteenth-century church of St Foteini, sole surviving church of a series of monuments in the valley, destroyed by the Ottoman governor for use in defence walls. The sounds of a howling child draw us down a deserted path where about 100 neatly dressed guests have gathered for a baptism, a major event in a Greek Orthodox family. Pausing to peer inside to witness an Orthodox baptism ceremony, we glimpse a world of silver and candles, the aroma of oil permeating the air. In the middle, a tall *pappas* in a long, embroidered, black cassock and surrounded by admiring relatives, immerses a screaming baby three times into a large baptismal font, symbolising the three days that Christ spent in the tomb. An honoured guest, a godparent, waiting to receive the baptised child, holds out a large, white towel to wrap the infant in.

As we tip-toe away from the private family occasion, the scent of almonds draws our eyes to a recessed display of traditional gifts and bundles of coloured, freshly sugared almonds and sweets. Easter desserts, wrapped in frilly pink tulle, and baptismal candles tied with satin ribbons, represent a 3000-year-old tradition and symbolise the hope that life will be blessed with more sweetness than bitterness.

Within a few metres of the church, cut into a rock, can be seen the bare cavern dedicated to Pan. Not far off, a short section of the Ilissos riverbed, which flows down from Hymettos, is just visible amongst shrubbery under a modern flyover. A strong reminder of what was one of two streams that flowed through Athens, this dried-up river patch evokes an area that was in the past both a holy precinct and a stretch of idyllic landscape.

We continue on our way eastwards towards a modern athletics track and the foundations of what was the most glorious church in Byzantine Athens. On an islet on the dried-up river, lies the ruined Ilissos Basilica, next to the tomb of the martyred Bishop Leonides of Athens, both closed to the public at the time of writing. Traditionally founded around 400, at the beginning of the Christian era by Empress Eudoxia, the basilica was built as a shrine to the bishop. The oldest, surviving remains of a Christian church in Athens, its walls and floor were decorated with marble and colourful mosaics of plants and birds. These remnants of carved decoration and detailed mosaic pavement, now in the Byzantine Museum, bear witness to what must have been a wonder for all to see and visit. In the museum's mosaic collection are displayed marble and glass decorations, combining Roman and Christian traditions from the entrance and sanctuary area of Ilissos Basilica.

Across the dual carriageway, on what was the north river bank, lie scant remains of the temple of Artemis Agrotera, Greek goddess of hunting and protector of women. The rural goddess was commemorated annually here with the sacrifice of 500 goats on the anniversary of the Battle of Marathon. Transformed into a Christian basilica in the fifth century, converted into a Roman Catholic chapel by the Venetians, it was rebuilt in the seventeenth century as the domed Blessed Virgin on the Rock (Panayia stin Petra). It was named, one tradition says, after a stone where Demeter, goddess of vegetation and farming, sat mourning the abduction of her daughter Persephone by the smitten Hades, Lord of the Underworld.

Further along from the basilica, on King Constantine Avenue, sits the Kallimarmaro, or 'beautifully marbled' stadium, home in 1896 of the revived, ancient Olympic Games. Celebration of the human body and athletics had been a central part of ancient religion, each event being devoted to a different god or goddess. Built for the athletic competitions of the Great Panathenaea, the greatest festivities in ancient Athens were held here. 300 oxen were sacrificed before the goddess's altar. Events included foot racing, jumping, horse and chariot races, wrestling and javelin throwing. Bronzed, stripped athletes aimed for one of the highest honours of the ancient Greek world – to be the winner in a Greek religious athletic contest, earning the esteem of fellow countrymen and the award of a laurel wreath. Gymnastics, an *essential* preparation for life, entailed a strong disciplined mind, and physical and spiritual perfection of the body, and was deemed crucial to defend the city.

The 50,000-seater, modern stadium was rebuilt in the mid-second century by Herodes Atticus. At the end of the nineteenth century it was remodelled by the Alexandrian Greek benefactor, George Averoff, and coincided with the growing popularity of athletic competitions across Europe. Set in a natural hollow next to pine-sloped Ardettos, the structure under the Romans was used for gladiatorial contests and wild beast shows. Remains of an underground tunnel at the far end indicate a passageway used by a thousand animals introduced by Hadrian and slaughtered here for Athenians' entertainment. Closed by a portico with mosaic-floored side rooms, the stadium with its Doric colonnade was described by Pausanius as a glory to behold. Entered by a bridge erected over the river for the crowds to enter in March 1896, the Kallimarmaro held the first officially recognised Olympic Games since the banning of pagan practices by Emperor Theodosius I in 393/4.

We cross Vasilissis Olgas Avenue towards the Zappeion exhibition buildings, once used for fencing competitions of the revived Olympic Games, and now a meeting place of the Council of Europe. Cutting into the gardens, drawn by the continuous hum of Athenians lingering over coffee, we take a break at the garden café, treating ourselves to coffee and yoghurt with honey syrup and cinnamon, before venturing up Irodhou Attikou, past the Presidential palace, towards the Byzantine Museum.

~~~

Before reaching Vasilissis Sophias, we turn right into Rigilis to look for the foundations of the wrestling school and Lyceum of Aristotle, the great fourth-century-BC philosopher. Built within a sanctuary to Apollo, the site included a gymnasium, military and athletic training facilities and an area for meetings of the Athenian Assembly. Having studied at Plato's Academy in the mid-fourth century BC, and served as a private tutor in Macedonia to the young Alexander the Great, Aristotle returned to Athens and taught at the lyceum before founding, in 334 BC, the Peripatetic School of Philosophy. After visiting the scant remains, we turn right up Vasilissis

Sophias towards the Byzantine Museum.

~~~

The Byzantine Museum

Constructed in 1848 over an aristocrat's villa on the banks of the Ilissos, part of the courtyard entrance of the museum is made up of late Roman pavement mosaics.

Tracing the rise of art from the ancient Greek world to the twentieth centuries, the Byzantine Museum, with multilevel underground galleries, exhibits architectural and devotional objects from Christianised temples throughout the Byzantine and post-Byzantine worlds. Rooms laid out like Byzantine churches include an early Christian basilica, a typical mid-Byzantine cruciform church, and a post-Byzantine single-aisle chapel. All three adaptations demonstrate the gradual changes in church interiors over the centuries, revealing the transformation of the ancient Greek spirit into an expression of deep spirituality. A collection of 3500 icons, an integral part of the Orthodox faith, are exhibited alongside sculptural decoration of churches including the converted Christian Parthenon and Erechtheion. Illuminated manuscripts, fragments of frescoes, mosaics, sarcophagi and artefacts of everyday life illustrate how the Christian church absorbed pagan symbols.

Individual items of interest are the fourth-century marble statues, The Good Shepherd, and Orpheus Playing a Lyre to Animals. Noteworthy is the marble relief, Virgin Hodegetria ('Leader'), from Thessaloniki, an eleventh-century marble slab with a relief tree of life between lions. Noteworthy mosaic icons of the Virgin Mary and Child, frescoes and artefacts representing the empire's one-thousand-year history and the post-Byzantine period are: the thirteenth-century double-sided icon of St George (one side painted, the other sculpted) and the mosaic icon of the *Virgin Glycophilousa* (Sweetly Kissing Virgin), brought over by refugees from Asia Minor in 1922; many fourteenth-century, double-sided, processional icons of the Virgin Hodegetria from Constantinople workshops; and a full-length Franco-Byzantine wall-painting of St Catherine. Not to be missed are: the fourteenth-century, gold and silver embroidered, three-panelled epitaphios from Thessaloniki, depicting the Lamentation over the Body of Christ; eighteenth-century mosaic of the *Virgin Galaktotrophousa* (Mary Breastfeeding her Child); post-Byzantine wall paintings including seventeenth-century frescoes from the church of Episcopi and St Andrew's convent; and the Franco-Byzantine *Virgin of the Catalans*, found in the ruins of St Elijah Church in the Athenian Agora.

7. Byzantine Athens

Making our way from Syntagma down through the chaos of Mitropoleos Street towards the cathedral, we come to the small seventeenth-century chapel of the Divine Power (Ayia Dynamis), related to Mary as protector of women in childbirth. Dedicated to the birth of the Virgin, Ayia Dynamis was built with a surrounding courtyard during Ottoman rule and served at one point as an ammunition depot for both Greeks and Turks. Set back off the narrow pavement, crouched between the pillars of a modern ministry in downtown Athens, the church brings to mind a dolls' house that has managed to survive against all the odds.

Dodging innumerable, parked cars and motorcycles, we step down through a tiny porch into a brightly lit room, its peaceful intimacy contrasting with sounding car horns and the stench of diesel emanating from bumper-to-bumper traffic outside. A paved floor displays a large double-headed eagle, symbol of the Byzantine emperors. Brasses gleam and metal-covered icons twinkle on a large, carved iconostasis, the screen displaying icons of church feasts. An old pappas, bearded Orthodox priest, bustles about. With hat perched high on his silver-haired bun, folds of his black vestments billow behind him. He appears kindly, unbothered by inessentials. Blackened wall paintings of saints, eaten away by time, once vivid colours illuminated by flickering candlelight, dress the walls. We can just make out St Philothei, martyred Athenian nun and founder of the monastery to St Andrew. A young worshipper wanders in, pausing to cross herself and kiss selected icons, before lighting candles and passing back into the world outside. It is the Orthodox Holy Week and residents are preparing to celebrate the Resurrection, supreme festival of the Eastern church.

Back outside, the pungent aroma of chargrilled lamb and peppers fills the air. *'Kalos irthate'* 'Welcome back!' calls the waiter with a long, raffish moustache, as we pass a small garden taverna. Treading our way carefully along the narrow sidepath, dodging parked motorcycles and cars, we come to Mitropoleos Square and Athens Cathedral, seat of the Orthodox archbishop. The twin towers of this huge building (Great Mitropolis) rear against the backdrop of modern Athens. Central point for the Greek Orthodox church, the cathedral was founded in 1834 when Athens, with a population of about 20,000, became the capital of new Greece. Planned by the Bavarian architect Ernst Ziller, the cornerstone was laid by King Otto and Queen Amalia in 1842 and took twenty years to build. With its mixture of neoclassical and neo-

Byzantine styles, the Great Mitropolis Cathedral epitomises the post-independence Byzantine revival.

Dedicated to the Annunciation of the Virgin, this grand building was built from the marble of 72 demolished churches on the site of the convent of St Andrew. Originally planned to be near the university, it was finally decided to build the monument among the people of Athens in the centre of the old town, where a paved square was created. The Athenians were filled with pride at the creation of their new cathedral, which contains the relics of St Philothei and Gregory V, Patriarch of Constantinople, hanged during the Ottoman occupation and whose body was later recovered from the Bosphorus. The grand, triple-arched portico, surmounted by a mosaic of the Annunciation, towers above the entrance. In the middle of the square, surrounded by traditional cafeterias, stands a life-size bronze statue of martyred St Constantine, last Byzantine Emperor, alongside a statue of Archbishop Damaskinos, protector of Greek Jews during World War II.

In the corner of the square, in the shadow of the Great Mitropolis, sits the tiny, dainty cross-in-square church of the Little Metropolis, once the cathedral of Athens. The religious house was also known as Panayia Gorgoepikoos, Our Lady who Grants Requests Quickly, due to a miracle-working icon of the Mother of God. Traditionally founded by Empress Irene and built over the site of an old temple dedicated to an ancient goddess of childbirth, the church was part of a monastery that was destroyed during the War of Independence. During the Ottoman period Little

Mitropolis was attached to the house of the archbishops, who had been ousted by the Crusaders from the Acropolis. Too small to serve as a cathedral, it was abandoned in 1827 and some years later it was used to house Athens' first library.

An elegant, slender Athenian dome rises on a high drum above a double-light window. The lower walls, of smooth marble, are a warm ochre colour, whilst the upper walls are made up of 90 ancient and early Byzantine marble slabs which run all round the church.

At the west entrance, the marble door frame is incised with Roman capitals and Christian crosses. Eastern elements abound: a relief of lions, carved between the arms of a small Christian cross, sits just above the door, above a relief of early Byzantine birds and griffins. Higher up on the cornice, a fourth-century BC frieze depicts the Attic months, represented by pagan festivals and seasons with their zodiac symbols. A unique fragmented relief of the Panathenaic procession, the ship carrying Athena's peplos survives, partially obscured by the later addition of crosses. Built into this same façade is a Christian, carved tree of life, flanked on either side by an Egyptian-type, double sphinx relief with oriental ornament. To our left, on the north wall, sits part of an ancient relief of a naked figure standing between two crosses. Round on the right, the south wall of the church, can be found a rare, carved relic of the Athenian Frankish period – a Crusader coat of arms. Originally decorated throughout with marble and frescoes, one faded surviving fresco of the Virgin and Child remains in the apse and a thirteenth-century icon of

Bishop Michael Choniates hangs in the entrance.

Nearby in Philothei Street sits the small church of St Andrew, on the ruins of a monastery and basilica dedicated to the apostle. Appearing to Philothei in a dream, St Andrew asked her to found a monastery and she dedicated this particular one in Athens to him. Philothei was martyred in 1589, and the religious house and church were demolished at the end of the nineteenth century to make room for new Archbishop's offices. The faded but still poignant figure of St Philothei can be seen in fragments of wall paintings moved from the demolished convent to the Byzantine Museum.

Wandering along Philothei and Evangelistrias Streets, we pass glass-fronted ecclesiastical shops filled with religious objects. The interiors are packed with a variety of ecclesiastical clothing, *epitaphios* shrouds and white baptismal outfits. Nearby shine gold-plated, silver and enamelled, swinging censers, twelve bells on each censer representing the twelve apostles. Gold-plated crowns, brass cauldrons and oil lamps sparkle. Incense burners, inlaid brass bowls with trays, candle-holders and gold and silver-plated votive plaques depicting images of a relevant body part or a longed-for baby, lie alongside wooden frames and altar chalices. DVDs of the Greek Orthodox liturgy and chant are stacked alongside holy book covers and pocket prayer books.

Close by, half-way up the now pedestrianised, fashionably chic, shopping street of Ermou, dwarfed by shops and tall apartment blocks of the modern city, squats the small church of Kapnikarea. Part of the Turkish bazaar in the

Ottoman era, congested with traffic for decades, this now pedestrianised square is filled with strolling Athenians and salesmen. A trio of street musicians strum and sing old Greek melodies, whilst the air hums with the sounds of animated conversation from pavement cafeteria, where Athenians sit and people-watch with their *paréa*, or 'group' - the core of Greek life.

Dedicated to the Presentation of the Virgin Mary to the Temple, the twelfth-century stone and brick Kapnikarea, probably named after a tax-collecting sponsor, consists of two churches and was constructed on the ruins of an ancient temple. Built in the traditional, Athenian cross-in-square plan, with an octagonal dome supported by four Roman columns, the Kapnikarea is typical of the mid-Byzantine period. The adjoining smaller domed chapel of St Barbara, an early Christian saint and martyr added during the Ottoman period, became a meeting place for Greeks. Having escaped demolition after independence in the 1830s, amidst unrealised plans to create avenues up to the new palace, the Kapnikarea was handed over to the University of Athens (to which it now belongs) and restored.

Approaching the east façade of the church from Ermou, three domed apses with gable roofs 'reach up' towards the dome. Round to the west side, blank arcades unfold along the façade of the outer vestibule, ending in a two-columned side-portico, topped with a modern mosaic of Virgin and Child. The octagonal dome, each section adorned with arched single-light windows, rises rhythmically above the arches and clustered roofs below.

This rhythmic flow of Byzantine architecture, a harmonious merging of Hellenic grace and oriental spirituality, is described by Hatzidakis in his fascinating book *Byzantine Athens* (1961). The interior of the Kapnikarea is richly decorated with neo-Byzantine frescoes by the greatest icon-painter of modern Greece, Fotias Kontoglu.

As a diversion, we retrace our steps along Athinas and turn left before the central market into Evripidou, to look for the small single-nave basilica of St John of the Column (Ayios Ioannis Kolona), recognisable by a marble pillar protruding through its low tiled roof. Set in a small courtyard during the Byzantine period, on the site of a sanctuary to an ancient doctor, the chapel takes its name from the protruding Roman column. Within the sanctuary can be seen the lower part of the marble, to which were attached shreds of garments or multicoloured threads, representing the illnesses of those seeking cures. Tradition states that John the Baptist was credited as a healer of shivering fits and fevers. The worshipper believed he tied his illness to the marble, burying the fevers beneath the ground. The practice continued till recently: ex-votos still hang from the church walls and threads are tied round the post.

On 29th August, feast day of St John the Baptist, the little chapel and the courtyard are filled with worshippers, spilling out with expectation and hope into the surrounding neighbourhood.

Now, in need of sustenance, we turn our attention to nearby Psiri, an old neighbourhood gentrified with restaurants, ouzerie and night clubs, but still retaining its old labour roots. Managing to find a free place at a table, we order *mezes* of feta, olives and halva, a popular Middle-Eastern sweet, and wind down with tsipouro with ice.

8. Easter in Plaka

Emptied streets and the appearance of half-masts remind us that we are in Holy Week. Greeks are fasting, the period of mourning has begun and those Athenians remaining in the city are preparing for the candlelight vigil and Epitaph procession. The pealing of church bells can be heard throughout the city.

Our starting point for Plaka, 'Neighbourhood of the Gods', and its cluster of churches, is the Russian St Lykodimou Church on traffic-filled Philhellinou, a main artery out of the modern city. Named after a donor family and dedicated to the Holy Trinity, the church is the largest medieval monument of Athens. Built as a small chapel in 1045, within the city's defensive wall, and reconstructed after the War of Independence on what was open land, its impact against a backdrop of modern buildings and deafening traffic is dramatic. Erected on the site of an early Christian basilica, which in its turn had been built over a Roman bath, it became part of a Roman Catholic monastery, only to be later destroyed by an earthquake. The half-ruined church was taken over after independence by the Russian Government for their community, when the bell tower was added.

The tall, modern bell tower, donated by Tsar and Emperor Alexander II, emerges from behind pines. It towers over a wide octagonal drum rising over low roofs, its decorative brickwork recalling that of the Holy Apostles in the Agora. The entrance is dominated by an imposing three-portal façade, where churchgoers today are gathering in preparation for the Holy Friday service of Lamentation. Head-scarfed women and young children have been arriving with spring flowers to decorate the embroidered epitaphios the symbolic bier of Christ, which will receive the image of the body of Christ, removed from the cross above. At dusk, after the evening service, in an uplifting mourning procession, the bier will be carried on the shoulders of members of the congregation through the streets of the neighbourhood.

Inside the tall building, decorated throughout in nineteenth-century Russian Orthodox style, the decorated shrine and replica of the cross rest beneath the iconostasis. All round the church exterior runs an Alpha and Omega frieze, representing the sacred initials of Christ's name, signifying the eternal nature of Christ, as told in the Revelation.

Not far away stands the Anglican church of St Paul's. Dedicated to the apostle who spoke to the Athenians on the Areopagus, St Paul's is one of the first churches built for a foreign community post-independence. Constructed in Hymettan marble, it is a national focus for the English-speaking community and contains plaques and inscriptions dedicated to British philhellenes. The windows on the left and right of the entrance depict scenes of the Israelites entering the promised land and are dedicated to General Richard Church, Philhellene commander of Greek forces in the War of Independence.

Across the dual carriageway a paved path, Kydatheneion, leads down past the Museum of Greek Folk Art into Plaka, old Athens. Situated below the Acropolis, Plaka, with its narrow stepped passages, was the centre of Byzantine Athens and seat of the Turkish governor during Ottoman rule. Swamped with mass tourism in the 1970s, the area became a magnet for over-zealous modernisers and property speculators amidst a burgeoning scene of hotels and night clubs. Having over time lost much of its character and charm (and residents), campaigns to rescue the stricken neighbourhood led to the outlawing of amplified music and the eventual closure of many roads.

~~~

Now almost traffic-free, the enchantment of Plaka survives: narrow winding streets, steep scuffed footpaths, and cobbled passageways weaving round pastel-coloured houses with interior courtyards, outlived the Ottomans and post-liberation demolition. Nineteenth-century and twentieth-century dilapidated and restored neoclassical houses stand scattered throughout the neighbourhood. And history stirs: beneath the corner tavernas and glass-fronted souvenir shops lie the souls of nineteenth-century academics, politicians, men and women of the church, writers, poets and ordinary folk, who were to play their part in the liberation of Greece. Alongside these heroes, in the maze of narrow streets, are to be found a dozen or more surviving mid-Byzantine churches.

Just a short distance from St Paul's, down Kydatheneion past the Jewish Museum, sits the twelfth-century restored church of the Transfiguration of the Saviour, known as Ayia Sotira. Towards late afternoon locals sit outside chatting on hard-backed chairs in doorways; old men lean on walking sticks and on the street corner a long-time accordionist strums plaintive melodies. In the nearby *kafeneion* men role dice and huddle over backgammon boards, whilst groups of sauntering, well-heeled foreigners pass through the cobbled lanes, seeking a way to the Acropolis or some other delight. Moustached waiters rush about, balancing trays of *dolmades*, stuffed vine leaves, and *horiatiki*, Greek village salad, with retsina and tumblers of iced water. 'Acropoli?' - Up Up!' calls out one reassuringly, waving a fully-laden arm ever upwards.

Set in a garden of evergreens alongside ancient columns, a vine-covered arbour leads through orange trees to the church courtyard. Drawn by the sound of chanting, we slip through the modernised entrance into the incense-filled interior. The church, full of standing worshippers, exudes the warmth and intimacy of a close parish community. In the doorway the sacristan whispers to us that a memorial service is under way. Our eyes follow the nave beneath a large, suspended chandelier, symbol of light and the presence of God. Around the holy table clergy gather and lead the softly chanting worshippers, the splendour of the interior and mysterious chant slowly enveloping us.

As we leave the church an old sacristan plucks a sprig of sweet-smelling basil from a nearby window-sill and presses it into my hand. Said to have been found in the soil where the Holy Cross was discovered by Sts Constantine and Helen, the herb is used in the Orthodox church to prepare holy water. *'Nostimo'*, I mumble in appreciation. 'Sto Theo', 'Thank God, not me,' he replies, eyes twinkling. 'Oraia Ellada?' he adds questioningly. Yes, Greece is *very* beautiful, we agree.

Before leaving Plaka, we visit the minute fourteenth-century church, Transfiguration of the Saviour (Metamorphosis tou Sotirou), commonly known as Little Saviour (Sotiraki). Situated at the northern foot of the Acropolis, the tiny chapel was built during the Venetian period (1395-1453), when Athens was ruled by the Acciajuoli family. A four-columned cross-inscribed church, the building has the traditional grace and elegance of mid-Byzantine basilicas, made up of rough-looking masonry with traces of brickwork patterns round the drum of an elongated Athenian dome. Very small, with no entrance area, the altar is made from an early Christian capital. The enthusiastic key holder points us towards the small side chapel cut into the rock, dedicated to the Christian martyr, St Paraskevi.

Emerging from the church as twilight deepens, we make our way back down to the centre of Athens, in readiness for the commemoration of Holy Saturday.

~~~

The following day (Holy Saturday) the ringing of church bells draws us back to Plaka, along the narrow street of the Tripods, where Easter streamers swing from apartment windows. The sounds of hymn-singing between priest and choir draw us up a steep path towards the eleventh-century parish church of St Nikolaos Rangavas.

Just behind the pretty restored church façade, the rock of the Acropolis rises steeply. The custodian, who had on our last visit offered us refreshments in the church courtyard, proudly tells us that the church was erected by the family of Emperor Rangavas, whose palace was situated in this area. A four-columned, domed cross-in-square church of fine Byzantine brickwork, the exterior is faced with the traditional sculpted stone and red brick courses, creating a warm, colouristic effect. Proudly pointing out the ancient slabs of marble and the old Arabic script in the walls, our friend shows us a hardly visible line of the more recently added-on chapel and gallery. The arched windows are simply adorned, and traditional, decorative ornament runs round the church exterior. The pretty bell tower, the first to be built after independence, the first to ring at Easter after independence, was also the first to sound in the city at the end of World War II, when over 300,000 civilians died from famine alone in Athens and over 50,000 were executed.

We squeeze into the dark interior of the now densely packed church smelling of burning wax. Scores of candles emblazon the interior, illuminating silver and gold-encased icons. The faithful are gathering in the church for the Easter readings; over the heads of the standing, softly murmuring congregation, we can just see, raised below the iconostasis, the epitaphios,, enwreathed with white carnations and roses. Expectant worshippers, mumbling softly, press forward with their children to gaze at the decorated shrine and kiss the embroidered cloth.

Close by, down some steps, sits the little cruciform twelfth-century church of St John the Evangelist (Ayios Ioannis o Theologos). Built during the Frankish era, the chapel sits hidden, sandwiched on a steeply stepped area between a taverna and modern houses. Characteristic of the mid-Byzantine style, an elegant eight-sided Athenian dome with marble colonettes rises above traditional stone and brick walls. The small entrance door is crowned by an arched niche and pediment. Inside, two columns are graced with Roman capitals. Fragments of recently discovered wall paintings from the Frankish period line the walls. Few examples of Byzantine paintings have survived in the churches of Athens, but in the dome the stern figure of the Almighty is painted in the stylised and solemn Byzantine style. In the vaults are finely but boldly outlined richly coloured figures of Sts Constantine and Helen. The warm reds of the garments of a finely drawn military saint on horseback, and deep blue background of the Ascension on the vault and walls of the sanctuary, speak of the influence of 'Crusader art', as seen in icons at St Catherine's in Sinai.

~~~

As night begins to fall, swept along by a tide of enthusiasm, we follow a growing crowd up some steps, through a passageway on to narrow Erechtheus, and down more steps into the palmed garden of the monastery of the Holy Sepulchre, Virgin of the Tomb (Panayiou Tafou), now a dependency of the church of the Holy Sepulchre in Jerusalem. Founded by the wealthy Kolokinthis family, the religious house was built on the burial ground of the Byzantine Greek Palaiologos family, last ruling dynasty of the empire. The seventeenth-century, single nave basilica of the Healing Saints (Ayii Anargyri), with its Baroque-style interior, was built within the monastery courtyard at the beginning of the Ottoman era. According to tradition, an earlier church had been founded by the Athenian Empress Irene, whose family lived in the area.

It is now early evening when the faithful congregate outside the church in anticipation of the Easter Eve vigil. By late evening the steps and narrow passageways down to the paved courtyard and marble-columned porch, are packed with worshippers hoping to catch sight of the Holy Fire from Jerusalem. Cats huddle together, rummaging for scraps thrown down from a monastery window above. Neatly dressed children with their parents buy unlit candles or clutch paper lanterns, trying to push their way through the shuffling crowd to the lit doorway of the church, from where voices of the clergy resound through loudspeakers.

A feeling of mounting expectation gathers pace that will culminate in the candle-lighting midnight service and the announcement 'Christos Anesti!' 'He is Risen!' Accompanied by a surge of joy and exuberant bell-ringing, the candlelit procession, led by priests in gilded robes, and choir with banners held high, will re-enact the journey of the women round Christ's tomb and pass through the neighbourhood. Athenians will take the sacred candles home and rub their front door with a cross for long-lasting protection, before breaking the fast with traditional *Magiritsa* (lamb offal) soup, washed down with retsina, ahead of later, slow-cooked Easter lamb and garlic.

Unable to get into the church, due to the crowd, we go back on our tracks to eat at the Psaras Taverna (The Fisherman), on the stepped slope near St John the Evangelist Church. The wafting scent of *skordalia*, or Greek potato garlic, olive, lemon and parsley, and freshly grilled *marides*, very small fish, flows across our path. Following our noses and the strong aroma of freshly grilled crusty bread, we sit down to enjoy a spread of wine *mezedes* of olives, *taramasalata*, Greek cod's roe dip, and Greek cheeses.

9. The Modern Boulevards and Wonders of the National Museum

The long-held dream of turning Athens into a modern European capital to match the city's ancient glory was realised when Athens, a small market town, was chosen as capital of the new nation; the young King Otto called upon European architects to plan the most beautiful capital for a population of about 40,000. Their aim was to create a modern metropolis, preserving the memory of Classicism.

We begin our discovery of the new nation in Syntagma at the Hellenic Parliament and Tomb of the Unknown Soldier, which commemorates all those who have died for Greece. The enchanting Theodorakis lyric *To gelasto paidi* (The Jovial Boy) sounds from a distant amplifier across the square, as we make our way over towards the fine building. The Hellenic Parliament, former palace of the first king of Greece and subsequent King George I, is an austere but elegant neoclassical building designed when the capital of Greece was transferred from Nafplio to Athens in 1834. Converted into the Parliament building in 1932, the Parliament and adjoining tomb symbolise the national pride and identity of Greek people. The Presidential Guard, or Evzones, wear an ancient style skirt, the fustanella, evolving from the dress worn by the mountain tribes who fought the Ottomans for the independence of Greece. The white skirt, made up of four hundred pleats reflecting four centuries of Turkish rule, is accompanied by long white socks and shoes with large pompons. The red fez hat represents the bloodshed of the Revolution, black tassels symbolising the tears of bondage.

We continue down Panepestimiou (University Street), one of the main thoroughfares of the city, leading down to Omonia Square. Alongside creeping traffic, we pass international banks and jewellers, European patisserie and *frappé* bars, before chancing upon, on our right, a magnificent Renaissance style mansion, the family home of Heinrich Schliemann, philhellene archaeologist and founder of Troy and Mycenae. Designed in 1878 by Ernst Ziller, beautifier of the new Athens, the mansion was known as Iliou Melathron, or Palace of Troy. With a curving double stairway and balustrade stretching up to a two-storey façade of Ionian colonnades, this elegant building, only a five-minute walk from Syntagma, defined the new city. The interior, filled with mosaics inspired by the finds of Mycenae and paintings of Pompeii, now houses the Numismatic Museum. Tempted by the smell of fresh coffee, we stop to refresh at the Muses garden café behind the mansion, surrounded by Classical statuary and lemon trees. Three minutes away from the frenetic pace of Athenian life, we experience stillness and calm.

Moving on, we pass the Ophthalmology Clinic, designed in 1854, its attractive stone façade and fine wrought iron railings bearing witness to the intricate craftsmanship of both neoclassical and Byzantine-style artists. Past the Greek Archaeological Society, set up after Independence to recover the antiquities of Greece, on past the Catholic Cathedral of St Dionysios, we come to the neoclassical trilogy – the Hellenic Academy, University and the National Library, designed by the Danish Hansen brothers in the nineteenth century. All three buildings were constructed in Pentelic marble. Neoclassicism, a European movement reviving the Classical features and sculptural grace of ancient architecture, with its pure, sharp oppositions of light and shade and contrasting colours, blended with the landscape, Greek light and surrounding monuments. It confirmed the longed-for continuity of the ancient world in Modern Greece.

First we come to the Hellenic Academy of Athens, completed in 1859, the crowning achievement of Athenian neoclassicism and European Classical revival, which recognised that ancient Greece provided the best examples of ideal beauty. Set back off the busy road, the design of the most important institution of learning in Greece was inspired by the east six-columned portico of the Erechtheion. Set amongst roses and fruit trees, beneath the pine slopes of lower Lykabettos, the

Academy's central façade and two wings are adorned with Ionic columns, its pediments filled with multifigured sculptures depicting the birth of Athena. Colossal statues of the goddess armed with lance and shield, defender of the city, and Apollo playing his lyre, tower on either side of the entrance near seated statues of Plato and Socrates. Athena, patron of agriculture, art and the sciences is depicted on the wing pediments. Symbol of freedom, democracy and dignity, the style, giving the appearance of antiquity, conveyed the importance of the liberated, modern city.

In the centre of the trilogy stands the university, completed five years later than the Academy and set back amongst orange trees behind a fountained forecourt. The Ionic portico, inspired by that of the Propylaia on the Acropolis, contains multicoloured friezes of Greek art, education and mythology. Directly in front of the building stands a statue of William Gladstone, recognised for his services to Hellenism. In the forecourt stand statues of philologist Korais, and Kapodistrias, first governor of Greece and founder of the university. In front are the two martyrs – poet Rigas Feraios and Patriarch Gregory V of Constantinople – portrayed before muses, sciences, and philosophers gathered around King Otto. Two large sphinxes, symbols of wisdom, stand on top of the portico. The first of the trilogy to be built, the university marked the revival of the arts and sciences under the new king. Combining architecture, painting and sculpture in the style of an ancient temple, it marked a new era of freedom for the Greek nation.

Next door sits the National Library. First founded on the island of Aegina as part of an orphanage, the library moved to Athens in 1834, initially operating in the public bath in the Roman Forum and then in the abandoned Gorgoepikoos Church. Finally completed in 1902, based on the design of the Hephaisteion and faced with a Doric portico, the building has a monumental, curved twin staircase and two side wings, set amongst a cluster of cypress trees. The reading room is surrounded by elegant Ionic-style columns. Funded partly by donations from philhellenes and Greeks living abroad, it now houses around a million titles, including many illuminated manuscripts and first editions. Having rapidly outgrown the present building, the bulk of the library will be relocated to a new building on the Phaleron Bay "Delta" in 2016.

In need of a break to collect our thoughts, we stop off to eat at a traditional Greek taverna off Panepistimiou, before setting out in the direction of the National Museum.

~~~

The National Museum

The National Museum, founded at the end of the nineteenth century, holds the largest collection of Greek art in the world. A 15-minute walk from Omonia or a bus ride from the Cathedral of St Dionysios to the Polytechneion, the museum (which also houses the Epigraphical Museum) traces the evolution of ancient Greek culture from the Neolithic Age through the Archaic, Classical, Hellenistic and Roman periods to the fifth century AD. A four-hour visit allows a brief view of some notable exhibits, enough to obtain a glimpse of daily life from Mycenaean to Roman times. Key to appreciating the Greek world, the National Museum is an evocation of the Greek spirit, or genius.

Immediately facing the entrance hall are the Prehistoric Rooms, Rooms 4-6, exhibiting important pieces of Neolithic, Cycladic and Mycenaean art. A glowing mass of treasures illustrating the glittering Mycenaean culture, which reached the central and eastern Mediterranean and the Black Sea, excavated by Heinrich Schliemann and others, dominate Room 4. Royal shaft graves from Mycenae and other prehistoric sites reflect the power and wealth of the kings from the beginning of Mycenaean civilisation. The golden death mask, or the 'Mask of Agamemnon', Greek hero of Homer's *Iliad*, faces us. Dated to around 1580 BC, recent archaeological research dates the funeral mask to around 1700 BC, many centuries before the Trojan War. Adjacent exhibits include the cup of Nestor, the 'Warrior Vase' and a boar's tusk helmet resembling one described in the *Iliad*; gold vessels and diadems engraved with religious scenes; a gold foil cover for the body of a child; inlaid bronze daggers and ceremonial swords; ivories and Linear B tablets; a golden-horned Bull's Head; and the famed fifteenth-century BC golden Vaphio cups, depicting scenes of hunters taming wild bulls.

Rooms 5 and 6, to the left and right of the Mycenaean Hall, cover Neolithic pottery and tools from Attica, Central Greece and Troy. The Cycladic collection, in Room 6, contains material dating back to the third millennium, including third- and second-century figurines that inspired the twentieth-century artists Picasso and Henry Moore; particularly noteworthy is the seated Man Playing a Lyre, one of the earliest examples of surviving Greek sculpture.

The sculptural collections occupy 30 rooms on the ground floor, beginning with the earliest pieces in Room 7 and ending with the works of late antiquity in Room 33. Turning back to the entrance hall, we circle clockwise round the museum, starting from Room 7. In the centre of this room are displayed artefacts of the Geometric period including the clay Dipylon amphora dating from about 750 BC, a five-foot grave marker and one of the earliest Greek works of art showing the human figure, recovered from the Kerameikos cemetery in Athens.

Rooms 8-13 display Archaic monumental kouroi, statues and funerary monuments inspired by Greece's contact with Egypt and the Near East. In Room 8 stands the 3-metre-high Sounion Kouros of the late seventh century BC, a votive offering to Poseidon, found at the sea-god's temple at Cape Sounion. The sixth-century BC Attic Volomandra Kouros and Merenda Kore, in Room 10, and the stele of a young *doryphorus*, a spearbearer, in Room 11, all show the emerging Greek Classical style and the Greek sculptor's increasing artistry in making statues come alive. Room 13 contains the stele of a Young Warrior and a funerary monument, the heavily-built Anavyssos Kouros, with a particularly radiant smile, dated around 520 BC. The epitaph below poignantly reads:`Pause and lament by the tomb of dead Kroisos, whom furious Ares slew when he was fighting in the front line'. In the same room stands the 500 BC Aristodikos kouros, an Athenian aristocrat warrior, one of the last Archaic Athenian gravestones to have come down to us as, during the first half of the fourth century BC, Athenians were banned from setting up expensive funerary monuments in the Kerameikos.

Highlights of the Classical collection, in Rooms 14-28, include the famed bronze Poseidon, dated 460 BC, about to hurl a trident, in Room 15. Found in the 1920s in two pieces on the sea bed off Cape Artemision, the god's perfectly balanced body and self-confidence encapsulate idealised male beauty and strength, where God is seen as a physically perfect man. In the same room, on the left, stands the Eleusinian votive panel showing Demeter, Mother Earth, accompanied by her daughter, Persephone, giving the first ear of corn to mankind. The Varvakeion Athena, a small Roman copy of the Parthenon Athena by Phidias, stands at the end of Room 20. With a shield and snake in her left hand, a winged victory in her right, and a triple crest of winged horses and sphinxes on her head, one can only imagine the awesome nature of the original.

Rooms 16-28 are dominated by fifth-century BC funerary monuments from the Kerameikos and other grave sites. Scenes representing intimate family unions depict the deceased, traditionally on the right, shaking hands with a loved one. Room 16 holds an early fifth-century stele recovered from Salamis, portraying a deceased youth holding a bird, whilst bidding farewell, alongside his empty birdcage and grieving slave. Room 18 contains the late fifth-century BC stele of seated Hegeso, a delicate figure of unspoken grief, selecting a necklace from a box handed to her by a slave girl. Room 21 is dominated by the Hellenistic Artemision bronze horse and jockey, an expressive boy astride a large galloping horse, found in the sea with the bronze Poseidon. In the same room stands the Diadumenos, a copy of a lost fifth-century BC bronze athlete binding on his victory wreath.

Rooms 36-42, at the foot of the stairs, contain the bronze collection dating from the Geometric, Archaic and Early Classical periods. Displayed here are: the Antikythera Mechanism, an astronomical computer of around 150-100 BC; the Stathatos collection, exhibiting antiquities and jewellery from central Greece and Macedonia; and the Egyptian collections covering the Pre-dynastic period to the time of the Roman Empire.

In the upstairs galleries, finds and frescoes recently excavated on the volcanic island of Santorini are, at the time of writing, displayed in the Thera Room. The Pottery collection, in Rooms 49-56, covering both Attic and Corinthian vases, depicts the evolution of Greek painting and the development of ceramics from the Bronze Age to the emergence of Attic black-figure and red-figure pottery from the sixth to early fourth centuries BC. Six amphorae, once filled with olive oil and presented to the winners of the Panathenaic Games, are displayed in Room 56, and a recently added Minor Arts collection can be viewed in Rooms 57-63.

On the ground floor, Rooms 25-27 display votive reliefs

found in the Asklepion on the Acropolis, dedicated to the Greek god of healing. Room 28 displays sculpture of the Late Classical period. Amongst the statues in this room are the famed Antikythera Youth, found in fragments in an ancient shipwreck off the island of Antikythera, and the bronze Marathon Boy found in the sea off Marathon. At the far end of the same room stands a fourth-century, marble head of Hygeia, goddess of health and daughter of Asklepios, found in Arcadia.

Rooms 29-30 feature Hellenistic sculpture, dating from the death of Alexander the Great in 323 BC, and include the tousled bronze head of a philosopher with penetrating inlaid eyes and a humerous group, dated 100 BC, of a nude Aphrodite scolding Pan with a sandal, Eros fluttering overhead!

Rooms 31-33 contain sculptures from Greek workshops of the Roman period. A bronze equestrian statue (without the horse) of an older Emperor Augustus, first Roman Emperor, dominates Room 31. Nearby stands a massive portrait head of Emperor Hadrian alongside his favourite, Antinoos, and a bust of Herodes Atticus next to his favourite, Polydeukion, both found at Herodes' villa in Kifissia, north of Athens.

~~~

In need of a renewed source of strength, we turn right outside the museum along Iraklio and find a family-run taverna which serves a particularly tasty, home-cooked *moussaka* and delicacies from all over Greece.

From the university we slowly stroll along Stadiou and over to Klafthmonos Square, formerly Lamentation Square, where in the nineteenth century civil servants, on being told they had lost their jobs, would go and weep outside the Mint. On the left of the square, the Museum of the City of Athens, a former early residence of the royal couple Otto and Amalia, contains furnishings from the couple's early period in the city and collections of engravings and paintings of long-vanished Athenian landscapes by eighteenth-century and nineteenth-century travellers. Making our way over to the lower side of the square, past electrical shops and *fastfoodadika*, we stop at a pavement cafeteria. Contending with both exuberant waiters and hungry cats, we spot an archaic-looking church built in the traditional Greek cross form, constructed in brickwork and crowned by an octagonal dome. Sunken into the paved square, surrounded by modern Athens, unexpected, sits the eleventh-century church of Sts Theodores.

Once situated on dusty country lanes, this robust-looking church was dedicated to the two martyred, military saints Theodores. Situated beneath orange trees, a tall octagonal dome with a decorative drum rises above multiple russet-coloured roofs overhanging arched windows, enlivened by dogtooth ornament. Its heavily-proportioned but graceful rhythm is enhanced by the typical pattern of the Byzantine period. A frieze of animal and plant ornamentation runs round the church and Arabic script decoration with glazed clay plates is inserted into the walls. Large icons of military saints dress the interior.

Further along Stadiou (south of Klafthmonas and Syntagma Squares) sits the Old Parliament Building, in front of which stands an equestrian statue of Kolokotronis, leader of the Greek War of Independence.

~~~

Kolonaki

Returning to Panepistimiou, we branch off up narrow, now-pedestrianised Voucharestiou towards Kolonaki district. Passing specialised boutiques and 'haute couture', we reach Kolonaki, upmarket Athens, home of the elite and chic boutiques. In the plateia the old-style *kafeneion*, where local men sit daylong, reading the paper and discussing world events over Greek coffee, has gradually given way to the *café frappé* and *cappuccino freddo* of the international set. The British Council and Library still stand, albeit with a plate glass entrance, in the lower square, joined by a Marks & Spencer.

We pass the local bakers where a lingering smell of baked herbs mingles with passing snatches of Chanel and Guerlain. On past the elegant façades of Skoufa, we come to the neo-Byzantine Catholic Cathedral of St Dionysios the Areopagite, first bishop and patron saint of Athens. Constructed in the mid-nineteenth century, the church is dedicated to Dionysios, member of the Supreme Court who converted to Christianity on hearing the words of St. Paul. The imposing neo-Renaissance style exterior of the building and the interior stained-glass windows are fine examples of the nineteenth-century Byzantine revival.

Returning to the plateia, we stroll along Patriarchou Ioachim. Sounds and scents of the streets of old Athens resonate: chirring cicadas just audible above the traffic, *mamá* calling down from a jasmine-laced balcony, and shops filled with sweet spices. Dodging concierges hosing down their patches of pavement, we pass locals sitting in the doorways to their apartment blocks, discussing the latest goings-on. Housewives take their weekly walk to *laiki*, the local market. The lingering scent of oregano and tantalising aroma of *melitsanosalata*, aubergine soaked in olive oil, floats down from above. We are tempted by the fresh smell of *loukoumades* from a nearby pastry shop.

Briskly turning the corner at the Marasleion, we pass the high walls and cypresses of the British School. Walking on, we reach the Petraki Monastery and the main church of the Incorporeal Archangels, dating from the thirteenth century and one of the oldest and most important churches in Athens. Situated in the now densely populated Lykabettos area of Kolonaki, surrounded by embassies and museums, the community was named after a physician who financed the monastery's restoration in the seventeenth century. Having played a philanthropic role during the War of Independence, providing care for the needs of the local population, the twenty or so monks continue to play a major role in Greece. Works carried out in past wars and refugee crises are manifest in the development of many of the city's modern schools, institutions and hospitals, all having received large donations from the monastic community.

Set in a neatly manicured garden, the religious house is

built in the old Byzantine style, with minimal decoration. The outer entrance is part of a nineteenth-century extension, and only the three apses remain of the original eleventh-century church. The interior church walls are covered in post-Byzantine frescoes painted by the nationally renowned eighteenth-century artist, Giorgios Markou.

As dusk gradually descends over the slopes of Hymettos and the last shafts of sunlight strike the Acropolis, we take our leave of the Petraki and walk slowly back towards the teeming streets of the lower town.

10. Daphne Monastery Mosaics

Barely a thirty-minute bus ride from the city centre, the long-abandoned Daphne monastery stands 11 kilometres north-west of Athens just off the ancient Sacred Way. Along the original road, thousands of worshippers from Mycenaean times until the outlawing of pagan practices, made their way annually to the sanctuary of Eleusis, to take part in the ancient Mysteries of goddess Demeter.

First built in the sixth century by Emperor Justinian on the site of a temple to Apollo, Daphne monastery was said to have been named after the laurel Daphne, sacred plant of the ancient god. It was rebuilt in the eleventh century when Orthodoxy, under the Commenian dynasty, had triumphed over iconoclasm and patronage was growing amid a period of increasing humanism in art. The mural mosaics at Daphne, together with those of two other Greek monasteries of that period - Osios Loukas near Delphi and the Nea Moni on the island of Chios - were part of this revival.

After the Frankish conquest of Byzantium in 1204, the monastery was handed over to Cistercian monks and it became the ducal burial place. The Cistercians survived two and a half centuries until expelled by the Ottomans in 1460, when the building was set alight. The Orthodox monks returned to the monastery in the sixteenth century, but it was again abandoned during the War of Independence, since when it has been severely damaged by fire and earthquakes. Used subsequently as the base for Greek guerrilla captains, a Bavarian road garrison, a French battalion station, a psychiatric hospital and in 1887 an animal pen, it has been under restoration since the 1894 and, more recent 1999 earthquakes. Its survival must be considered no less than a miracle.

A local man accompanies us over the busy dual carriageway. 'Monastiri', he mumbles, his voice barely audible over the roar of juggernauts thundering towards the Eleusinian oil refineries. After waving us off in the direction of remote, thick pinewoods, we come to an isolated wrought iron gate. Here we are joined by a neatly coiffed Greek woman with her son and French daughter-in-law who, apparently fasting, offer us some homemade, Greek Easter bread. Insisting we take some home to enjoy with traditional, red-dyed eggs, she wraps some up for Laura while asking us about ourselves. Soon the *philakas* emerges.

At first glance the church appears to be on the point of demolition. Behind a high battlemented wall, the thick Byzantine walls of the church sit submerged in scaffolding near a cypress tree. Severely damaged in the 1999 earthquake, the entire church, exterior and interior, remains under restoration. Across the courtyard, ruins of a monks' refectory and a large well remind us that, for several hundred years, a thriving monastic community survived in this bleak terrain. Accompanied by a small group of visitors, the *philakas* explains that we will be able to see some, but not all, mosaics by climbing the restorers' scaffolding and that a film of the mosaics is available to watch in an adjoining room. Passing the cloisters, she ushers us through a plain doorway, its portico once adorned with four Ionic columns.

Inside the church we are transported into a mystical world, a miniature of the Universe. Light from the windows of the dome draws our attention upwards; our gaze follows the high walls and piers up towards the dome, from where the grave figure of the Almighty, looks down at us.

Below, in His presence, the laity, surrounded by life-size images of saints and stories from the gospels, participated in the divine liturgy and received the Eucharist, the body of Christ. The re-enactment of the major events of Christ's life in the church liturgy was depicted according to strict rules regarding the content of scenes and their positioning, both within the architectural framework of the church, and within the setting of lamps and candles. Familiarity with the traditional features of Byzantine art – the two-dimensional style, idealised figures, spiritualised faces, certain gestures and colours - enabled the Byzantine worshipper to come face to face with the holy person and experience his love. The glittering mosaics speak of the spiritual world and the strong sense of faith that created them. Created by skilled craftsmen, they consisted of thousands of hand-cut, opaque glass tiles or stones and gold leaf. Individual pieces were cut and angled in different positions on the plastered wall in order to catch the light at a variety of angles, the surface of the plastered wall itself varying in thickness. Yet, the gold that *we see* in Byzantine art, the Byzantines *experienced* as divine light.

In the muted light of the narthex, where the unbaptised remained during the liturgy, an atmosphere of pastoral delight greets us. The lower walls, once covered with vividly coloured marble panelling to complement the mosaics above, a Byzantine tradition developed in the courts of Constantinople, have been replaced by fading seventeenth-century murals. The upper walls are covered with Byzantine scenes of fanciful countryside, the mosaics depicting the life of the Virgin, to whom the monastery was dedicated. Unlike the more solemn mosaics of the basilica of S. Apollinaire Nuovo in Ravenna, the centre of late Roman mosaic art, or even those of the more contemporary Osios Loukas, these display movement and realism.

Against a gold background symbolising the light of God, St Ann and Joachim in *The Prayer* sit separated by a tree in a two-dimensional garden of pale green foliage, the pretty ornamental gold border intact. An angel enters in answer to Joachim's prayer. St Anne, in a pale pink robe prays, while a servant stands peering from a doorway as she draws back a curtain. In the *Presentation of the Virgin in the Temple*, young Mary, traditionally clothed in the oriental maphorion, Byzantine holy veil and symbol of the divine, is led by her parents to be blessed by priests.

Further along above the west entrance of the church grieving apostles are depicted in a fragmented *Dormition*. The Virgin reclines on a bed, her head just visible, dressed in a traditional, deep ultramarine blue robe, of the most precious and expensive pigment and scattered with gold stars, signifying purity. Standing at the head of the Virgin's bed, the subtly drawn expressive faces of the apostles reveal increasing individualism. An angel floats down, discreetly holding out a cloth to receive the soul of the mother of God.

Edging our way up the spiral scaffolding, past metal beams and platforms, we come face to face with mosaics of the higher spheres of the cosmos. Only partly visible from the scaffolding, narrative scenes from Christ's life adorn the upper walls and the four curved niches at the base of the cupola, speaking of a transcendent world. We are enveloped in an aura of light-reflecting mosaics that glorify the Christian God, the richness linking the decoration directly to the power of the Emperor and his court. In the sanctuary, on either side of the damaged mosaic of the *Virgin and Child*, on gold embroidered footstools, stand the figures of Archangels Michael and Gabriel, dressed in the luxurious costume of a Byzantine court, framed by a decorative border. Standing close by are life-size figures of eternal saints, reflecting the triumph of the Church. In the *Crucifixion*, the elongated figures and slightly gaunt facial features against the gold background display Egyptian influence, whilst the poignant, restrained grief of the Virgin and St John reveals a growing emphasis on human emotion and the Classical style, revived at the courts of Constantinople.

Above us, beneath the drum, in the niches, are depicted the major themes of Orthodox iconography: the *Annunciation, Nativity, Baptism* and the *Metamorphosis*. These many-figured compositions have progressed from the oriental, elongated imperial figures of those of St Sophia in Constantinople and St Vitale in Ravenna. These group portraits, with their graceful gestures, noble and realistic expressions, exude the spiritual grace of ancient sculpture.

Closer to the sanctuary, The Virgin in the *Annunciation* stands upright, looking pensive in an ultramarine blue mantle; the angel in flowing folds of chiton, an ancient Greek tunic, and himation, an ancient cloak thrown over the left shoulder, arms outstretched, moves forward like a Nike goddess, recalling the balance and harmony of the Classical style. Depicted on a plain gold surface of minutely cut tesserae, the scene shimmers with a mysterious intensity.

The half-perished image of the *Baptism* emerges from a brilliant gold background, symbolising eternal life. Lit by natural light from the windows of the dome above, a life-size figure of the naked Christ, at once luminous, stands facing us in the transparent waters of the River Jordan. A ray of light shines down from heaven, in which can be seen the hand of God and a descending dove, symbol of the Holy Spirit. The spiritualised expression of Christ with a finely drawn body resembling a Greek athlete, giving an illusion of slight movement, depicts a transitory moment. On the left, John the Baptist, with outstretched hand, leans forward and touches Christ's head; opposite him, angels, clutching blue and pink towels, lean forward in anticipation of Christ stepping from the cold water. The stiffness of the Christ of earlier mosaics has developed amid the growing mood of realism and warmth.

The Daphne mosaics, defined by nobility of feature and gesture with elegance, reveal this growing interest in realism in the, *Nativity*, where Mary and Joseph rest at the entrance of a rocky cave, while an ox and ass peer over the edge of the crib. Marvelling angels and shepherds hover in the background, while sheep drink from a stream. Classical inspiration is clearly seen in the pose of seated Joseph, his boldly outlined face and falling folds of drapery.

Realism is strongly manifest in the figure of Hades in the *Descent into Hell.* Christ, in chiton and himation, straddles the gates of hell, raising Adam and Eve; the figure of defeated Hades lies bound and gagged, semi-clothed, his body and pose recalling the anatomy of an ancient River God.

The *Transfiguration* depicts the radiant apparition of Christ in a blue mandorla symbolising the light and luminescence of the glory of God, to his disciples. In the light of the church window, the figure of Christ seems to project towards us, whilst those of the prophets Elias and Moses stand near him. Down below, on rocky landscape, the awakening apostles react in different ways: Peter, kneeling, looks up to Christ, John faints, whilst James is waking. In the earliest known mosaic of the *Transfiguration* - the sixth-century version at St Catherine's in Sinai - the figures are more stylised and remote from each other, but here the group are interacting, made all the more intense by the positioning of the glittering tesserae on the receding edge of the curve. Communicating both with each other and with us, the awakening apostles encompass us in their shock and amazement. Higher up and in towards the dome we confront the sixteen prophets, some dressed in oriental robes and others in the Classical style, each one standing between windows at the base of the dome, foretelling the Incarnation.

At the top, above the saints and prophets, the imposing figure of Christ Pantocrator, all-seeing, looks down at us from the shimmering gold heavens. Christ clutches the jewelled gospel with His left hand, blessing with the right. His concern for mankind, for us, is emphasised by the dark, arched eyebrows and dogged lines on the forehead. Christ's spiritual power is expressed in His large furrowed eyes, pupils thoughtfully turned sideways, looking into the distance, whilst at the same time focusing on us. Dressed in a garment of blue, colour of the Redeemer, an awesome but compassionate Christ judges our acts.

Slowly descending the scaffold, we turn and look back at the Daphne mosaics. A combination of Hellenistic, Roman and Eastern art, the mosaics incorporate the Classical line and sense of beauty of Hellenism with the spirituality of Byzantium. Leaving behind a world of glory, a place touched by eternity, we make our way back to the bright lights of the city.

References

1. M. Choniates, *Inaugural Address,* quoted A. Kaldellis, *The Christian Parthenon,* N.Y., 2009, p.159.

2. N. da Martoni, *Pilgrimage Book,* quoted M. Beard, *The Parthenon,* London, 2010pp. 60-61.

3. M. Beard,op.cit. p.66.

4. Dankoff, R. & Kim, S., *An Ottoman Traveller,* London, 2010, pp.281-6.

Bibliography

American School of Classical
Studies at Athens, *Garden Lore of Ancient Athens* Athenian Agora Picture Book 8, Princeton, 1963.
Barber, Robin (ed.), *Athens: Blue Guide*, London, 2002.
Bastea, Eleni, *The Creation of Modern Athens*, Cambridge, 2000.
Beard, Mary, *The Parthenon*, London, 2010.
Birley Anthony, *Hadrian, the Restless Emperor*, London, 1997.
Bouras, Haralambos *et al.*, *Athens from the Classical Period until Today*, Athens, 2003.
Bowra, C.M., *Periclean Athens*, Harmondsworth, 1974.
Brown, Peter, *The Cult of the Saints*, Chicago, 1982.
Byron, Robert, *The Byzantine Achievement: an historical perspective* London, 1987
Camp, John M., *The Archaeology of Athens*, New Haven/London, 2001.
Chandler, R., *Travels in Asia Minor and Greece*, Oxford, 1825
Cormack, R & Vassilaki, M., (eds.), *Byzantium; 330-1543*, London Royal Academy of Arts, Exhibition Cat., 2008.
Dankoff, R & Kim, S (eds.), *An Ottoman Traveller: Selections from the Book of Travels of Evliya Chelebi*, London, 2010.
Decastro, Marisa, *Seven Walks Through Athens: A Guide for Young People*, Athens, 2010
Dimitrakopoulos, D., *Ekklisies kai Monastiria ton Athinon*, Athens, 2006.
Enisleidou, C, M., *H Pantanassa ton Athinon*, Athens,

Fox, David Scott,	1966. *Mediterranean Heritage*, London, 1978.
Freely, John,	*Strolling Through Athens*, London, 2004.
Goette, Hans Rupprecht,	*Athens, Attica and the Megarid; an Archaeological Guide*, London, 2001.
Gombrich, Ernst,	*The Story of Art*, Oxford, 1989.
Gough, Michael,	*The Origins of Christian Art*, London, 1973.
Graves, Robert,	*Greek Myths*, London, 1981.
Hatzidakis, Manoles,	*Byzantine Athens*, Athens, 1961
Hatzidakis, Nano,	Mosaics and Wall-Paintings in Byzantine & post-Byzantine Churches in *Athens*, ed. Bouras *et al*, 2003
Herbert, Michael,	*Daphni: A Guide to the Mosaics and their Inscriptions*, London, 1978.
Herodotus(ed.)P.Cartledge,	T*he Histories*.Tom Holland (trans.), New York, 2014.
Herrin, Judith,	*Byzantium*, Harmondsworth,2008.
Hetherington, Paul,	*Byzantine and Medieval Greece, Churches, Castles and Art*, London, 1991.
Kairophylas, Ioannis,	*Stis Plakas tis Anephories*, Athens, 2007.
Kaldellis, Anthony,	*The Christian Parthenon*, New York, 2009.
Kaltsas, Nikolaos,	*The National Archaeological Museum*, Athens, 2007.
Kazantzakis, Nikos,	*Travels in Greece (Journey to the Morea)*. F.A. Reed (trans.), Oxford, 1966
Kitto, H.D.F.,	*The Greeks*, Harmondsworth, 1951.
Krautheimer, Richard,	Early Christian and Byzantine

	Architecture, Harmondsworth, 1975.
Lidderdale, H.A.,(ed.),	M*akriyiannis: the memoirs of General Makriyiannis 1797-1864*, Oxford, 1966.
Llewellyn Smith, Michael,	*Olympics in Athens 1896 – The Invention of the Modern Olympic Games*, London, 2004.
MacKendrick, Paul,	*The Greek Stones Speak*, London, 1962.
Mango, Cyril,	*Byzantine Architecture*, London, 1979.
Micheli, Lisa,	*Unknown Athens*, Athens, 1990.
Millar, Fergus,	*A Greek Roman Empire; Power and Belief under Theodosius II (408–450)*, Berkeley, California, 2006.
Miller, Henry,	*The Colossus of Maroussi*, Chichester, 2007.
Morton, H.V.,	*In the Steps of St. Paul*, London, 1937.
Pausanius,	*Guide to Greece*. Peter Levi (trans.), London, 1971
Pentreath, Guy,	*Hellenic Traveller*, London, 1987.
Plutarch, "Pericles",	*The Rise and Fall of Athens*. Ian Scott-Kilvert(trans.), London,1973
Powell, Dilys,	*Remember Greece*, London, 1941.
Rice, David Talbot,	*The Art of the Byzantine* Era, London, 1994.
Rice, Tamara Talbot,	*Everyday Life in Byzantium*, London, 1967.
Richter, G.M.,	*A Handbook of Greek Art*, London, 1959.
Rupp, David,	*Peripatoi: Athenian Walks*, Athens, 2004.
Runciman, Steven,	*Byzantine Style and Civilization* Harmondsworth, 1975.

Setton, K.M.,	*Athens in the Middle Ages*, London, 1975.
Sicilianos, D.,	*Old and New Athens,* London, 1960.
Speller, Elizabeth,	*Following Hadrian,* London, 2002.
Stobart, J.C.,	*The Glory that was Greece*, London, 1964
Ware, Timothy,	*The Orthodox Church*, Harmondsworth, 1980.
Waterfield, Robin,	*Athens: A History*, London, 2004.
Wheler, George,	*Journey into Greece,* London, 1682.

Photographic Sources

Photographs are reproduced courtesy of commons.wikimedia.org.

1. Acropolis, CC-BY-SA 2.5
2. Mask of Agamemnon, CC-BY-SA 2.0 (National Archaeological Museum/ Photographer: Xuan Che)
3. The Parthenon in Athens, CC-BY-SA 2.0 (Photographer: Steve Swayne)
4. Porch of Maidens, CC BY-SA 2.5
5. Dionysos pediment Parthenon BM – (Elgin Collection), CC-BY-SA 2.5 (Photographer Marie-Lan Nguyen)
6. Cavalcade west frieze Parthenon BM – (Elgin Collection)
7. Kerameikos 2 Athens, CC BY SA 4.0
8. ACMA Moschophorus CC BY-SA 2.5 (Photographer Marsyas)
9. Theatre of Dionysos, CC-BY-SA 3.0 (Acropolis South slope)
10. Socrates by Leonidas Drosis, Athens – Academy of Athens (Detail) CC-BY-SA 3.0
11. NAMA – Herakles and Nessos by Nessos painter, CC-BY-SA 2.5 (National Archaeological Museum, Athens)
12. Mount Lykabettus, by Greenshed
13. Athens-dekadrachm-1, Classical Numismatic Group, Inc.www.cngcoins.com
14. Adriano 5, CC-BY-SA 30 (National Archaeological Museum Athens/Photographer R.A. Frantz)
15. Attica 06-13 Athens 21, View from Acropolis Museum – Agia Apostoli, CC-BY-SA 2.0 (Photographer A. Savin)
16. 2155 Byzantine Museum, Athens – St Michael (14th century), CC-BY-SAA 2.0 (Photographer G.Ddallorto)
17. Monastiraki Square, Athens
18. Bundesarchiv, Bild 183-771706-0030, CC-BY-SA 3.0
19. Athens Plaka 07, by JF Kennedy at English Wikipedia
20. Louis entering Kallimarmaron at the 1896 Athens Olympics
21. Changing of the Guard, Athens (13), CC BY SA 30

Every effort has been made to trace copyright holders; it is hoped that any omission will be excused.

The Author

Helen Partovi-Fraser has lived and worked in Athens as a tutor, and has visited all the places she writes about. She is a former teacher, has studied Art History and worked in hospitals. After a period away from the rapidly changing city, she returned to Athens with her daughter in 2013, to rediscover its secrets.